LETTERS TO NOBODY

LETTERS TO NOBODY

1908-1913

BY THE

RT. HON. SIR GUY FLEETWOOD WILSON

G. C. I. E., K. C. B., K. C. M. G.

GYAN

Published by

GYAN

Gyan Publishing House
5, Ansari Road
Daryaganj, New Delhi-110002
Phone: 011-47034999, 9811692060
E-mail: books@gyanbooks.com

Distribution Network
gyanbooks.com
India, USA, Canada, UK, Australia, France

ISBN: 978-81-212-8220-8 (PB)
First Published, 1921

2nd Impression 2023

Printed at: Gyan Press, Delhi.

LETTERS TO NOBODY
Author: SIR GUY FLEETWOOD WILSON

LETTERS TO NOBODY

Photo: Maull and Fox.

Guy Fleetwood Wilson

LETTERS TO NOBODY

1908–1913

BY THE

RT. HON. SIR GUY FLEETWOOD WILSON

G.C.I.E., K.C.B., K.C.M.G.

WITH PORTRAIT AND ILLUSTRATIONS

LONDON

JOHN MURRAY, ALBEMARLE STREET, W. 1

1921

AFFECTIONATELY DEDICATED TO
MY GOOD FRIENDS THE SIMLA MONKEYS,
WHOSE ENTERTAINING COMPANIONSHIP HELPED TO STEM
MANY A WAVE OF OVERWHELMING DEPRESSION,
AND WHO SEEMED TO UNDERSTAND ME AS
I THINK I UNDERSTOOD THEM

CONTENTS

LIST OF ILLUSTRATIONS

LETTERS TO NOBODY

LETTER I.—ARRIVAL

CALCUTTA, *November 29th*, 1908.

HERE am I, having survived a journey which for me has been a genuine delight, and having survived also the fellow-passengers on the P. and O. Some proved to be attractive and friendly, the rest, the major portion, assumed a critical attitude undisguised and distinctly unfavourable. These decided and asserted:

1. That I have a wife and four children, that I maltreat the first and neglect the rest.

2. That I suffer from cancer, and that one year in India will kill me.

3. That I have been removed from the public service of the Crown in England, and that I have been jobbed into the position I now hold by my uncle, John Morley. He is no relation. If he were, I should proudly claim him as such, for he is the ablest, the most far-seeing, and the strongest Secretary of State who has ever presided at the India Office.

4. That I am hopelessly incompetent and altogether unfit to be Finance Minister in India.

As to 4, I am not altogether disinclined to agree with them.

I already realise that what is wanted is unimpaired health, which I have not got; greater youth than I possess; an even temper and you know that mine is a garment which hangs somewhat loosely about my shoulders; a large fund of patience, which I hope to develop; and an ability to which I lay no claim. But I realise also that all, English and Indian, are disposed to give me a "run for my money," a fair chance, and if loving the country, loving the people, loving the heat, and loving my work can compensate for the lack of other requisite qualities, I may perchance not altogether fail.

LETTER II.—FIRST TIGERS

SUNDERBUNDS, *New Year's Eve*, 1908.

I HAD been but a very few weeks in India when, almost by accident, I heard of a good tiger in this locality and decided *coûte que coûte* to try to get him.

I approached the Viceroy in some trepidation, as the New Year dinner is an important official function which all members of Council are expected to attend.

I think His Excellency already realises that on some points he and I are not likely to see eye to eye, and this made it all the more difficult for me to ask a somewhat indiscreet favour.

But I had known him in former years as Melgund, and have already realised that the old charm, the old sweetness of disposition, and, above all, the old sporting instinct are still to the fore. The qualities which make it impossible not to feel genuine affection for Lord Minto seem to have developed rather than shrunk, and my request was granted not only readily, but very gracefully.

Mr. Meyer, the Agent to the Nawab of Dacca, most kindly arranged it all, and Mackenzie, the Secretary of the U.S. Club, equally kindly saw to the food and drink for me. We left Calcutta on Sunday night at 10.30, and reached Koolna at 4 a.m. on Monday—bitterly cold. We took the jute-carrying steamer and steamed all day through a feverish country but a most interesting one. The main river, the Barisal, is broad and swift, the banks on each side being dense bamboo jungle. I had a good bath in a large half-barrel, and we ate our own food. At Jallacarti we found Meyer in a most marvellous paddle-launch built in the year one for the Nawab. They gave me his cabin, and I have been quite comfortable. We have a house-boat in tow on which the other four men live—Charles Mackenzie, Meyer, Pulford (an officer of the Gurkhas), and Mr. Jack the Commissioner—all nice men. We have been after tiger on Tuesday, Wednesday, and Thursday, but done no good. It is very interesting and perhaps somewhat risky work. We rig up three bamboos like a tripod, and tie cross-bits to sit upon. The whole thing is somewhat frail, and only 9 or 10 feet from the ground. The *machâns*, as they are called, are put in a row at the head of a jungle, just as you post guns in pheasant-shooting. A crowd of natives then start at the opposite end, and advance through the covert with rattles which make the most hideous noise. They also light and throw into the jungle small crackers called by the rather grand name of bombs. The tiger, if there be one, either slinks out from the side of the covert, or, if he is a "dangerous" one, waits till the last moment, and then charges with a roar either back on the beaters or, usually, straight on ahead. If he charges out, he passes like a flash, and it is quick and difficult shooting. If he "backs," it is seldom one gets a shot at him at all.

Tigers are getting very rare anywhere near

centres like Calcutta, and the only reason why there are any left in the Sunderbunds is because men do not like to take the risk of fever. I am afraid I shall not see one. I have only one day left. I have shot a big crocodile and seen one big pig (wild-boar) and a fine stag, but had to let them go by, as we hoped for tiger. I must leave off now, as we have heard rumours of a tiger, and the launch is starting. It is a great business: a regular fleet of native boats with *machâns*, beaters, and my body-guard of seven Gurkhas—quite unnecessary, I think, but this is the centre of Bengal unrest, and I found the Gurkha police awaiting me.

January 1st.—I have had a grand day. I have shot two tigers. One is an unusually fine one, with beautiful markings and great breadth of body. The other, his wife, is a bit smaller. I can hardly realise yet that I really have got two good tigers within seven weeks of landing in India. I am hugely pleased and right glad that I shot straight. I hit the big one just into the left shoulder, and the tigress right through the heart and lungs. They both lay dead within some 6 or 8 feet of where I hit them. I was perched up in my *machân* at the edge of a clearing, and just saying to myself how easy it would be for a tiger to sweep the whole thing away, when I saw the head of a big tiger pushing through a thick round bush. I could hardly believe my eyes. It was just like a scene of "jungle life in India" which one sees in fancy pictures in the illustrated papers. I caught his eye just as I saw him, and I realised that there was not a moment to spare. I aimed at his shoulder and pulled. He roared, stood straight up on his hind-legs, and began to box with his fore-legs. It was a grand sight. He then fell back and died, poor old boy! I was just getting down from the *machân*, and the beaters were beginning to gather together in the open, when the second tiger, of which no one knew anything, dashed out with a roar, her tail lashing right and left and her mouth wide open. She seemed to be in a vile temper and inclined to charge the *machân*, up which a native was trying to climb, but swerved. I gave her a shot and caught her behind the shoulder. She roared, sprang into the air and went a regular header into a thick bush, and then died.

It has been a most exciting and successful New Year's Day, and I shall return to Calcutta to-morrow a happier man. I was the only one who got a chance, and I think I may say that I have not thrown it away. But I got the chance chiefly owing to the unselfishness of my companions, who insisted on giving me the best place and the first shots.

Many, many men are years in India without ever seeing a tiger, and I have got two already. The natives were delighted and the Gurkhas nearly beside themselves. They are very keen sports-men. The *bandobast*—that is, the whole thing—was admirably arranged. So far as I can make out, I am none the worse for it, and I think it is worth running some risk of fever to get a couple of tigers. But it is a feverish place, and one might come once too often.

I enjoyed all the bird life and the absolutely

Photo: C. A. Mackenzie, Esq.

A RIGHT AND LEFT—SUNDERBUNDS.

wild India of the Sunderbunds. It is quite unlike anything I have seen before. Not nearly so beautiful as many other places, but singularly wild and uncanny. The heat was severe, and I found sitting on the *machân* during the hottest time of the day, in a scorching sun without shade of any sort, very trying. Once or twice I had to walk four or five miles over paddy-fields in the blazing sun and felt rather queer. I am old for this game, but I revel in heat and love the sun, and have scraped through without a touch of fever. What struck me most was everyone's utter indifference to the fact that tigers were within a couple of hundred yards of us. We never even took the rifles out of their covers, and all the men who built the *machâns* were quite unconcerned. I suggested that at least one of us should load and keep a look-out; but my friends smiled and said no tiger ever dreamed of charging unless disturbed and angered. I suppose they know all about it. Be that as it may, tiger-shooting is the king of sport, and I am glad indeed to have taken part in it.

I shall arrive at Calcutta on Sunday, January 3rd, 1909, having left on the previous Sunday night. Forty hours' journey each way—and a right and left at tigers.

LETTER III.—LEGISLATIVE COUNCIL SESSION, 1909

CALCUTTA, *April*, 1909.

THE Legislative Council Session ended on March 29th, and I have felt like a carp flung on the grass to gasp out its life ever since.

I promised to tell you how I got through my first Session, and I will proceed to fulfil my promise.

For me the two salient features of the last Session of the "old style Council" have been the detestable, but I fear unavoidable, repressive legislation and the financial deficit inherited from my predecessors.

I feel sure that I shall soon learn to love India, and I am reconciled to the severance of ties in England, but I have already had one great and disagreeable surprise. I have never in the past studied Indian affairs, and I had no conception that unrest and the poison of sedition had eaten into a section of the Indian community. The fact has become somewhat pronounced of late, and I have been looking into the past.

I find that last June, before I landed in India, it was considered necessary to introduce a Bill in the Legislative Council to enable the Government of India to control explosives, and the Member for Home Affairs, in giving his reasons for the measure, stated:

"The nature of the danger which we have to meet has been revealed in the recent attempts to derail by explosive bombs the train of the Lieutenant-Governor of Bengal, in the attempt on the life of the Maire de Chandernagore, in the terrible murders of two ladies at Muzaffarpur, in the discovery of a bomb factory in Calcutta, in the subsequent attempt to destroy a tramcar, and in the deposit of a bomb of great power in the precincts of a church."

On the same occasion the Home Member introduced a Bill dealing with Incitements to Murder in Newspapers. I have seen a few of the papers which seem to have made such legislation necessary, and their tone certainly seems to me to have been indefensible. Much as I detest meddling with the freedom of the Press, I can well conceive that some of the articles in the Native Press of a certain class are calculated to do immeasurable harm amongst the young, impressionable, and somewhat emotional Bengalis. The chief danger appears to me to lie in the fact that the articles are almost always an astute admixture of sedition, mysticism, and religion.

I came out fully anticipating possibly grave financial difficulties and anxieties, but I certainly never realised that I should be called upon to support repressive legislation of somewhat drastic character. I already realise that two things will be essential—cool-headedness and scrupulous regard for what I may term very placid justice.

What I dislike is this shower of repressive measures which are being introduced.

We have had also a Criminal Law Amendment

Bill introduced at the first Legislative Council Meeting which I have attended.

The events which influenced the Government in bringing forward the measure are the following:

On December 6th, 1907, an attempt was made to assassinate the Lieutenant-Governor of Bengal by means of a bomb exploded under his train near Midnapore. Two other abortive attempts of a similar nature on Sir Andrew Fraser's life had already been made on the railway-line near Chandernagore. On December 23rd, 1907, Mr. Allen, the District Magistrate of Dacca, was shot with a revolver at Goalundo. On March 4th, 1908, Mr. Hickenbotham of the Church Missionary Society was shot near his house at Kushtia. On April 11th an attempt was made to assassinate the Mayor of Chandernagore by a bomb. On April 30th a bomb intended for Mr. Kingsford, who had been Presidency Magistrate at Calcutta, was thrown into a carriage at Muzaffarpur, and killed Mr. and Miss Kennedy. On May 2nd the Manicktolla bomb conspiracy was brought to light. On June 2nd a serious dacoity was committed near Nawabganj, in Dacca District, by a large band armed with guns and revolvers, in which two persons were killed. On June 21st a bomb was thrown into a railway-carriage at Kankanara and injured an English gentleman, and there have been several similar attempts in the same neighbourhood. On August 31st an approver in the Manicktolla case, which is under trial at Alipur, was murdered. On September 17th a serious dacoity was committed at Serampore. On October 20th and 30th similar dacoities were committed in Malda and Faridpore Districts. Only a few days ago followed a dacoity of the gravest nature in Raita. There is ample reason for believing that all of the dacoities which I have mentioned were committed by young men of the middle classes. On September 23rd a young man was convicted of sending a bomb by post to the Magistrate of Nadia. On November 7th the fourth attempt was made to assassinate the Lieutenant-Governor of Bengal, on this occasion with a revolver. On November 9th the Native Sub-Inspector of Police, who had arrested one of the Muzaffarpur murderers, was shot dead in the streets of Calcutta. On November 13th the principal witness in a case against the head of an association called the Anusilan Samiti was murdered and decapitated near Dacca.

I am afraid the necessity for the Bill has been made out. The sad part of the whole business is that the seditious and dangerous element is an infinitesimal fraction of the Indian people, but the misconduct looms large in the public mind, and there arises a tendency to forget the wholly admirable conduct of the population as a whole.

What has already struck me is the even temper and fairness with which the Indian members deal with what must be for them unpalatable legislation. It certainly is so to me, necessary though it be, and it threatens to march hand in hand with my financial anxieties, to which I shall now invite your attention.

I had been assured in London that I might expect parity at the end of the year 1909-10, but I had not been six weeks in Calcutta before I found out that the year would pass out with a heavy deficit; I had to frame my Budget at short notice and try to make two ends meet without adding to taxation.

We are told that you cannot make bricks without straw, but the bricks were made, and so was my Budget.

I introduced my Financial Statement for 1909-10 on March 22nd, 1909, and a very unpleasant Statement it devolved on me to make.

I explained to a sleepy Assembly (the heat was unbearable) that the past year had been an unfortunate one. It had begun with famine in four provinces and a partial famine in the three others. That excessive malaria and bad trade had accompanied a very poor harvest, and that the net result of the year's finance (for which I was not responsible) was a deficit of no less than £3,700,000—the first deficit since the year 1897-8.

I managed to frame a Budget for the coming year which showed a small surplus without any additional taxation.

After me followed every member of the Council endowed with ideas or the lack thereof. Also the grievance-mongers.

The Indians are impatient of the large allotments to the Army and the railways. They would like to see the money spent on irrigation and education.

But the Morley reforms have put them in good-humour, and they accorded me marked courtesy and consideration, and, I think, general approval.

The Gladstone of debate is quite evidently Mr. Gokhale. A severe critic, a somewhat habitual fault-finder, he is none the less as fair as he is forcible.

Eloquent and incisive, he would be a great orator but for a pedagogue's tone and manner. His speech covered thirteen foolscap pages of close print, and he traversed the whole field of Indian affairs. I cannot complain of his treatment of me or of my financial proposals.

The speech which constituted the chief interest of the Budget debate was Kitchener's.

Lord Kitchener detests speaking in public and is an unusually bad speaker, but as the speech had been carefully prepared, and as he read every word of it, the effect was good. It will be his last speech in the Council of India.

It is a speech calculated to render me, quite unintentionally, very great service, for it lays down the principle that the Commander-in-Chief is solely answerable for the Army vote and for the proper expenditure under it.

In his opening sentence he said:

"The present Budget is, in several respects, exceptional, marking something of an epoch in military finance. In the first place, it is the only military Budget framed since I have been in India under circumstances of general financial stringency. In previous years the revenues of this country have been in such a prosperous condition that it was wise to place, out of our abundance, a certain amount to reserve by improving our military security. But, just as strongly as I hold that to have been a wise policy, so I consider that, under the present straitened circumstances, military expenditure should be kept as low as possible whilst duly providing for the maintenance of the present state of efficiency in the Army."

As I am sure to be charged with starving the Army, this remark will prove very helpful. His second sentence is even of greater value to me, as it defines the power and personal responsibility of the Commander-in-Chief for the financial administration of the Army:

"This Budget debate has a special importance of its own; for it is the first time that a member of Your Excellency's Government has addressed this Council, charged, under Your Excellency's orders, with undivided responsibility for both the efficiency and the economical administration of the Army in India."

He then proceeded to render an account of his stewardship during his tenure of office, and he certainly established a just claim for long and faithful service in India.

I would add "and invaluable" but for the fact he has, in my opinion, taken far too much into his own hands, and created a "one-man" administration which, minus its creator, is likely to crumble to pieces.

The more I see of Kitchener the more I am disposed to call him "the man of contradictions." I am convinced that he would gladly be burned at the stake rather than save his life at the cost of a lie. Of this I am confident. But to get the best of a deal in the interest of his country, I have known him lie like the proverbial trooper.

I well remember, when I was his Financial Adviser during the South African War, the effrontery with which he gained his point when driving a bargain with a transport company. He had determined to cancel one of the appalling "agreements," which Lord Roberts (the antithesis of Kitchener as regards expenditure) had effected during his command.

I told him that the agreement, however disastrous to public funds, was quite *en règle* and must be respected.

He asked me to be present at the conference with the company's officials, but extracted a promise that I would not utter one word from first to last.

After playing with his adversaries as a cat with a mouse, and with extra velvety paws, he sighed and, pointing to me, said: " I don't like to insist, but there sits a gentleman sent out by the Government to order me to withdraw all protection from your property unless you agree to review this agreement." And he got his way.

I remained speechless, not only during, but for long after, the termination of the conference!

Another " contradiction " is his scrupulous observance of a financial undertaking and his barefaced readiness to repudiate an engagement in which no money is involved.

I experienced this more than once in South Africa. Kitchener cabled to the Government and asked that I should be sent out. I was Assistant Under-Secretary of State for War at the time, and retained that rank whilst abroad, so that I was in a large measure independent of him.

From first to last we got on splendidly, and I have nothing but very pleasant recollections of our association, but just at first I had one severe tussle with him.

We had come to an understanding that if what

he wanted done was done as I advised, I should sign the decision and be responsible for it.

On the other hand, if he insisted on doing a thing his own way, he was to sign or initial the document and bear the burden as regards result.

The first time there was trouble was when he refused to initial his instructions, and denied ever having agreed to do so.

Eventually he yielded and appended his initials in pencil, but so faintly that the result was quasi-invisible.

My temper flared up. I stepped up to his writing-table, seized his gum-pot, and laid a good dab of gum on his signature. "Why on earth do you do that?" said K. "Because," I replied, "the initial will show through the gum, and you will not be able to rub it off."

I never had any trouble with him again.

Taking him all round, as the saying is, I think he is about the biggest living Englishman, and I can truthfully say, "Perfidious K., with all thy faults I love thee still."

I am grieved that his time in India is up.

It devolved on me to wind up the debate, and I did so at, I fear, inordinate length. I will inflict on you only my concluding sentence:

"The reforms which have been decided upon, and which will presumably become operative before this time next year, will unquestionably vastly increase the labour and the difficulties of the Finance Member.

"I do not fear the change.

"Undoubtedly it will lead to increased and more searching criticism, but I believe that the criticism will be the outcome, not of an intention to embarrass a public servant who is honestly trying to do his duty, but rather of a desire to help him to effect improvement.

"I shall welcome criticism because I believe my critics will be actuated by the same impulse, the same desire, which will influence me—a common desire to improve the work of those who govern and the condition of those who have to bear taxation."

I now know what a jelly-fish feels when he melts away on the sand in the sun.

LETTER IV.—SAMBHALPUR, HARDA, DELHI, AND PETERHOF

SIMLA, *April 23rd*, 1909.

I PRESENTED my Budget Statement on the last day of March, and for six weeks previously I can honestly say that I worked twelve hours out of the twenty-four under very trying conditions. The weather in Calcutta in March is always very trying; very hot and very damp. This year it was abnormally bad, and there was a great deal of sickness in consequence. Work under these circumstances was exceptionally trying, and I must confess that it was an enormous relief to me to get into the train and turn my back on the capital of India, although on the whole I cannot say that I dislike Calcutta. Indeed, personally, I should be quite prepared to live there all the year round if I had two clear months' leave during the worst season of the year.

I left Calcutta on April 1st, and went into the Central Province in the hope of getting tiger. I reached Sambhalpur on the 2nd, and was met by the Deputy-Commissioner, a charming man of the name of Moberly, who kindly ran my camp for me and did all he could to find me sport. I had to drive twenty-eight miles along a road part of which had been washed away, and I did not reach the camp till late at night. The position of the camp was beautiful. It was in an opening in the heart of the jungle with three fine large mawa-trees which gave us welcome shade. The heat in the Central Province, on the edge of which I was, even in April, is intense, and I again came in for abnormal weather. I believe the thermometer varied from 108° to 116°. I was promptly covered with prickly heat; but I never felt better in my life and thoroughly enjoyed the heat. I sat on the *machân* exposed to the full strength of the sun for many hours a day; but, thanks to a spine protector and an enormous sun-helmet, I am none the worse for it. I have had bad luck as regards sport. I ought to have got three tigers. They came nearly within shooting distance, and on each occasion turned round and broke through the beaters. One tigress had three beautiful young cubs and she would have made short work of anyone who stood in her way. The beaters wisely climbed trees and let her pass. The second tiger was coming straight for me, when it was turned by a number of chattering monkeys which swarmed about the trees around me, and made such a noise that the tiger turned and got through the beaters. The third tiger was also coming straight for me, but it was turned by a beater who, unknown to me, had climbed into a tree close beside me, and who had a bad fit of coughing, probably attributable to excitement, just as the tiger was coming. This tiger also broke through the beaters, so that I have not yet added to my Christmas bag. I got one black bear and lost a second, although it was badly wounded. It got into a large cave and no one could go in after it. It would have been too dangerous, as the opening was very small and the cave pitch dark.

On the 8th of April I left Sambhalpur with great regret and reached Harda on the 10th. There I stayed with a retired merchant who has built himself a bungalow in the heart of the jungle, and was kindness itself. In his day he was a great shikari, having killed twenty tigers with his own rifle in the Sunderbunds alone. The district seems to me to have been cleared out of game by strolling officers. I tried to get a good sambhur, but saw nothing but young stags, and the old ones had shed their horns. I saw a nylghai bull, but he also was, in my opinion, too young to shoot. I do not care to shoot anything unless it is worth shooting, and for that reason I let off two beautiful half-grown leopard cubs which came close to my *machân*, and literally played around it like two kittens. It was one of the prettiest sights I ever saw. I got one big black bear, a very fine specimen, and that is all I have been able to do in the way of sport.

Previously I had had rather an exciting time of it over a large she-bear which Moberly wounded badly. She had four small cubs, and after going a considerable distance, took up a position inside a large hole on the side of a hill. Moberly was above and I was below the bear. I took my rifle from the bearer, and then to my vexation found that the man who carried my cartridges had vanished, and I was in the pleasant position of being within 10 yards of an angry, wounded she-bear, showing every inclination to charge me. I had nothing but my knife. Fortunately she would not leave her cubs, and that gave Moberly time to come round and kill her. The four little cubs were not bigger than spaniels and would not leave their mother. To my great distress, the beaters rushed in and killed them before we could interfere. They detest bears, as they so often get mauled by them. It is rare for a man to be hurt by a tiger, but it is of common occurrence for the cultivators to be badly mauled by bears. Indeed, we went after the she-bear because she had only the day before attacked a man and nearly gnawed his hand and arm off. We patched him up as best we could and sent him in to Sambhalpur. The wretched man had to be carried twenty-eight miles on a charpoi, or bed, in the broiling heat of the sun. I went to see him in hospital on my way back, and he seemed to me to be in a bad way. Another man was mauled by a bear. We doctored him as best we could; but we had nothing with us but Pond's Extract, which, however, is an excellent remedy for almost everything.

The charm of the real jungle, such as you get in the Central Province, is beyond what any words can describe. A *machân* is just high enough to prevent one's being seen or smelt; but it is low enough to enable one to see everything, and to watch even tiny little creatures such as mouse-deer, which are not larger than a pug dog. But one has to sit for hours as immovable as a heron on one leg in shallow water waiting to strike a fish. The least movement makes everything look up and then vanish.

First of all there are the monkeys, the veritable Banderlog of Rudyard Kipling. I detest monkeys in captivity, but wild they are a source of perennial joy. I almost forgave the troop which cost me my tiger, they were so diverting: wise-looking old ones, flighty young ones, babies all on the jump, literally, and all hopelessly idiotic. A monkey is a human idiot, only more human.

When they turned my tiger, they looked at my glasses and said to each other, " What a funny old monkey this is! He has got glass eyes"; and they stared and jabbered till one of them missed his hold and had a heavy fall, whereat they all shrieked with terribly human laughter and tore away, leaping from tree to tree. Quite the Banderlog. Then come the peacocks, any number of them, strutting about followed by their peahens. They look superb when flying through the air high above the trees. The small birds are very beautiful. One finds oneself surrounded by golden oreoles, blue jays, black-and-white minas, brilliant kingfishers, and any number of little dots of life and colour.

When one is after tiger, one may not, of course, fire at anything else, so wild-boar, bear, leopard, and every kind of deer pass by quite unaware of one's existence and showing themselves under perfectly natural conditions.

I had the chance, a rare one, of seeing a whole family of hunting dogs. Papa was, alas! shot by another gun, but Mamma and four puppies passed right under me, so frightened, so tired, so hot, with long, wet, red tongues hanging out. They were mixed up with a wolf and a jackal, which is very unusual.

The jungle itself is not beautiful. It is too

burnt up and thirsty-looking. I prefer the mud and bamboo Sunderbunds to the red dusty ground, the sparse trees, and burnt-up shrubs of the Central Province. But the life is far greater and more diversified in the latter jungle. I verily believe that if I remained long in India I should dwell in the jungle and never kill another living thing.

At Sambhalpur I had to do twenty-eight miles on a pad elephant, the most unpleasant mode of progression I know except a bullock tonga, and in a bullock tonga at Harda I had to do eighty miles on a forest track. When I reached the train, and for some days afterwards, I felt as though every bone in my body were broken.

On my way from Harda to Simla I stayed at Delhi—quite the most interesting place I have yet seen in India. It is difficult to visit all the spots connected with the Mutiny and to stand by Nicholson's grave without emotion. The palace is singularly beautiful, and quite the best and very ornate part of it is the work of an Italian who worked in the service of a King of Delhi. The King, it is said, put his eyes out as soon as he had finished his work, to prevent his doing similar work for anyone else in India.

I reached Simla on the 22nd. From heat at 110° or thereabouts I found myself in mid-winter, pitiless cold, rain, incessant storms, and quite the most detestable weather I have ever experienced even in England. It seems to be improving now, but up to the present I have felt the cold intensely, especially coming, as I have, into a large and empty house.

Peterhof is like a large, well-planned English

country-house. There is a ball-room, a billiard-room, a dining-room where I could dine forty-two people, and a very large double drawing-room. Some of the rooms are panelled, regardless of cost, with Indian walnut, and the furniture is, or was, the best that money can buy. On the other hand, nearly every fireplace smokes and not a door or window closes properly. But that is indeed India all over. I think the recent outlay on this house is indefensible, and personally, as Finance Minister, I should never have agreed to it. It used to be the Viceregal Lodge, and was inhabited by Lord Lytton, Lord Ripon, Lord Dufferin, and Lord Lansdowne. I must say that it is a very attractive house, and the terraced garden, which is of quite good size, with beautiful creepers and very nice trees, is not only a great attraction but an enormous comfort to me. I am training the wild monkeys to come and feed in the garden, much to my gardener's despair. They certainly are very destructive. The jackals come in at night, and the birds are beginning to get quite tame. As you know, I love to have living things about the place. The number of offers I have had from the gentler sex to come and stay in Peterhof and run the house for me would astonish you. But I have already acquired the reputation of being a cross-grained old bachelor, a reputation which I shall do my best to keep up.

I found heavy arrears of work, which, however, I hope to get through before H.E. the Viceroy arrives on the 1st, as I want to have a clear desk before the new work begins. I do not mind the work, but what I really dread is the social hard

Photo: E. W. Baker, Esq., I.S.O.

PETERHOF, SIMLA.

labour of Simla. They seem to me to be absolutely mad on the subject of social functions in this country. It seems to be one incessant round of garden-parties, dinners, and dances. I do not think, however, that they will get me to go out much in Simla any more than they did in Calcutta.

I was very glad indeed to get your letter, and shall always be grateful whenever you write to me, as I cannot but feel very much alone, removed as I am from all my old friends and English associations, although I must say I have received much kindness and consideration since I landed in India.

Since my arrival here I have not had time to look round, my whole days being taken up in putting the house straight and unpacking my worldly goods from England. I am glad I brought many of my things from England. Most of the shops here are dear and the stuff is bad, and although bringing things from England entails great trouble and some extra expense, on the whole I think it is the better plan.

I have been unfortunate in one respect. The earthquake of last October caused a great crack in the main chimney-shaft of the house, and the first fire lighted nearly burned down Peterhof. All the carpets and some of the floors have had to come up, and I have experienced all the misery inseparable from builders, bricks and mortar, dust and dirt, to say nothing of being unable to light fires. But things are getting straight, and I hope soon to settle down for the first time since I landed in India.

LETTER V.—KASHMIR

SIMLA, *October 4th*, 1909.

A BAD hand and arm from the bite of a wild monkey and strained muscles of my back, thanks to my pony bucking more than usual, made me feel so sorry for myself that I was advised to take a couple of weeks off. I have not stirred from Simla since April and not missed a day at the office since then, and I felt I needed a change. I hardened my heart and started for the Rawalpindi frontier and Kashmir. I knew Lady Younghusband as a girl, and she has often asked me to visit them. I left Simla at 12 on September 26th, and had the usual weary six hours' journey to Kalka, which I have already done four times.

At Dharampore we passed a Sikh regiment on the march—on trek, as one used to say in South Africa. It was a picturesque sight, and the only one except a covey of wild peacocks disturbed by the train.

I got to Umballa at night and to Lahore in the early morning. The heat was severe, and by me quite unexpected. I felt it acutely, as I was autumn dressed. I travel in great luxury, but even a Finance Minister cannot lay the dust, and the dust is awful.

From Lahore onwards for hours and hours I travelled through the most magnificent crops.

The plain is absolutely flat, well wooded, and fairly well watered. On one sandy section there seemed to be a camel farm, for I saw over a hundred, and very well they looked.

Between Lahore and Wazirabad we crossed the Jhelum River, wider than the Thames at Westminster. It is the irrigator of the Punjab. If anything can save me from a deficit this year it will be the harvest. The country I have been through looked like a very fertile district in France. All highly cultivated and the crops superb. The only danger is a shortage of labour through malaria, of which there is an ominous threatening.

At Jhelum the river widens out into a broad lake, and from Jhelum to Rawalpindi the train climbs slowly and tediously through a curious country which looks as though giant children had been making giant pies all over it. I am told it is the result of two sand-storms meeting and bunching up the sand driven by the wind from opposite directions.

It seemed quite arid and the heat was oppressive. Gradually one rises into more mountainous country, rocks taking the place of mounds.

At Rawalpindi I was able to hire, utterly regardless of cost, a De Dion motor with quite the best driver I ever sat behind—a Punjabi. We left Rawalpindi at 4.30 and got as far as Murree, where I had to pass the night in an indifferent hotel-bungalow. I had to start again at 6.45 a.m., and had one of the most tiring days I ever remember. We travelled for fifteen hours at a stretch over the worst road I ever knew a motor attempt. I stopped at Baramulla and got some tea, petrol, and carbide for the lamps; and that is all the rest I had. I was very tired when I got to Srinagar (pronounced (Srinugger), which is the summer capital of Kashmir, at 9.30 p.m. I was kindly, nay warmly, received by Sir Francis and Lady Younghusband, and most comfortably housed into the bargain. The road into Kashmir runs through a country singularly like the finest part of Perthshire, till you get into the finer and wider part, where it is more like the Pyrenees. The Jhelum borders the road nearly the whole way, and is a grand sight this year owing to the great volume of water. The floods have been phenomenal in Kashmir, and much of the country is still under water. One feature of this place is the extraordinary growth of Lombardy poplars. They are superb, and line each side of the road for some thirty miles. Between Baramulla and Srinagar the road is quite flat, but between Murree and Baramulla it is hilly and almost impassable at present owing to landslips and huge bits of rocks which have rolled on to the road from the mountain-tops.

When I tell you that, besides this, the road has hardly any parapet, that there is a fall of some hundred feet on one side, and that it is crowded with troops of mules, donkeys, and camels, with strings of bullock carts, and that children, goats, and dogs stroll about quite unconcerned, you will realise that motoring has its terrors in Kashmir. The country hereabouts is quite unlike what I expected. First of all, it is quite hot; secondly, it is quite flat; thirdly, it is quite civilised. I expected Kashmir goats on rocks, fierce men with long match-locks, and something akin to savagery all round. Bless you, one might be in a provincial town in the South of France!

There is something very reposeful and attractive about it all, but it is not what I expected. Next day I had a look round, and in the afternoon was taken to see the Volunteer prize-giving in a swampy, chilly field. I received a visit from the Rajah of Tickin, who seems a cheery young man, and who asked me to shoot tiger with him in January.

I called on the Maharajah of Kashmir, who received me in Durbar in a large hall, elaborately painted like a Turkish bath. I was made acquainted with all his Ministers, who seem exceptionally nice, intelligent men. I also called on the Rajah of Punch (pronounced Poonch), who gives huge bear drives, and who has very good mahser-fishing. He asked me to indulge in both, but I have not time. They returned my visit the same afternoon. The Maharajah of Kashmir is my age, short and rather stout. I have found him most pleasant and very intelligent. He arranged a shoot for me in camp.

On Friday I started for the camp, which was placed in a lovely spot in the mountains, fifteen miles up, all of which I had to do on a hill pony. I was very tired and glad to turn into my tent soon after arrival. The camp was beautifully "done" and the beating, etc., admirable, but the shoot was not a success. I worked like a slave for three days, Saturday, Sunday, and Monday, and saw nothing but one small bear cub which ran about in the grass, and which I am really glad to have missed. He was much too small. I was up at 5 each morning, and rode and walked up and down mountains all day, getting into camp between 8 and 9 at night.

On the third day I was "on the go" for sixteen solid hours and rode thirty-two miles. It was not wise to work so hard, but I had set my heart on shooting a barasingha, which is the giant stag of Kashmir. But there is really not much game left. The country has been shot out, and no sensible man will select Kashmir merely to shoot in. On Tuesday I rode into Srinagar, very done up, to attend a garden-party kindly given by the Maharajah in my honour at a villa in beautiful gardens with countless fountains. There was a band and all the officials attended, and we had a gigantic banquet of sweets. The Maharajah was greatly upset when I told him I had not seen any game, and insisted on my going shooting again on Tuesday next. A great show for the morrow (Wednesday) in the shape of a cricket match.

The great cricket event of the year is over. I attended the match, and to my surprise found myself sitting next to Kapurthala's Spanish wife, who looked very sweet and very lovely. He was in great form. He had been up in the mountains for ten days and had not fired a shot. We groused together.

The cricket was truly wonderful, and the Maharajah of Kashmir was duly credited with fifty runs. His side made 330 runs!

Now for the expedition. I had to leave at 6 in the State motor and drive twenty-five miles. Then I got on a horse and began a laborious and, as it turned out, a dangerous climb towards the top of a high mountain. Instead of giving me a tat, or hill pony, the Maharajah did me the honour to mount me on a curveting peacocky charger, with a long tail and little else to recommend him. I did not like to object, but I "had me doots" when I started. We had got about two-thirds up the mountain and I was in front of the party, when my steed shied, reared, and over we went. It was the work of a second, but it seemed a lifetime. The horse stood for a second straight up on his hind-legs, then he reared, fell back, and bounded like a ball over and over some 200 feet down the side, half of which was perpendicular, and was smashed to pieces on the rocks at the bottom. When he reared I jerked my feet out of the stirrups, cast away the bridle, and tried to slip off to one side. I succeeded, but I was over the edge myself, and the horse fell all but on the top of me. His side just touched my head. Then I began to slide faster and faster to certain death. I lay quite still on my back and slid faster and faster: All I could do was to spread my legs wide apart, make my heels scrape as much as possible, and spread out my fingers and use my poor nails as claws. Still I went faster and faster. Just as I thought it was to be one quick shoot and death, my heels caught a ridge of grass. I dug my nails into a little loose earth and grass and stopped. I think that was the most trying time I have ever known in my life. I could see between my toes an almost sheer fall of a hundred feet on to the rocks below. I felt the little tufts of grass give, give, give, and I almost regretted not having gone down at first. It was all a question of time. Mercifully the shikaris were Punjabis. They are *real men.* With their sticks they made little nicks on the mountain-side for their toes and fingers, and at last—it did seem ages—they reached me, and slowly and very carefully we all got up to the top, over the ledge, and on to the path. At the moment I did not feel even shaken. Ames and Chaplin of the Indian Cavalry were out with me and looked green. They said it was most trying to see me go over, slide away, and then hold on to a little grass, and to be unable to help me. It really was worse for them than for me. What I disliked most was having to walk up the mountain for two hours in a broiling sun to show them that I was really unhurt. To satisfy them as to my nerves I made a gallery shot at a musk deer and rolled him over.

We had 800 beaters and a huge drive, and all I saw was an inch of a stag's neck. I fired and hit it. He bled, but was in my opinion not badly wounded, and I may lose him.

I had to crawl down the mountain, ride ten miles on the flat, and motor twenty-five miles home. I got to the Residency at 10.30, and there found the Maharajah waiting for me in a terrible state. He had made up his mind that I had been killed. I was much touched by his quite obviously genuine distress.

I found also a telegram calling me at once to Simla, and I had to start for Rawalpindi at 6 a.m.

I had a hopeless Eurasian driver who ran into a cow and nearly sent us down into the river, but I caught the train and repeated my journey between Rawalpindi and Simla. I seem to have done a good deal in a very short time.

I am very glad to have seen the Kashmir-Gilit frontier. From a strategical standpoint it was most interesting, and the frontier officers are a fine body of men.

The Younghusbands were kindness itself, and his account of his mission to Tibet was beyond words interesting. I had long and most enlightening talks with him and like him immensely.

I felt nothing till to-day, but now I feel very sore and shaken. I have loosened a tooth, which hurts me, and I have no nails left, no skin on my nose, and my cigarette-case is smashed flat. But after a couple of days of the simple life I shall be quite myself again. I feel very sorry for the poor horse; he must have had a terrible two minutes.

LETTER VI.—THE KYBER, SIRMOOR, AND BENARES

CALCUTTA, *November 18th*, 1909.

I HAVE been doing my cold weather tour *en route* to Calcutta. I went first to Srinagar. It was a great trial to have to run back to Simla from Kashmir for just one meeting of Council, as it meant doing the whole journey to Rawalpindi over again. Hot, dusty, and very wearisome. Peshawar is a few hours beyond Rawalpindi. I am very glad, however, that I went, as I have been able to see the Afghanistan frontier and visit the Kyber and other places I have heard so much about, and which to an Anglo-Indian, as I now am, are of surpassing interest. I got there on Thursday, the 28th, and stayed with the Chief Commissioner, Sir George Roos-Keppel. He seems to me a clever, thoughtful man. The house is nice and comfortable, but terribly hot. Indeed, the heat all along the frontier is cruel. It surprised me. On Friday I visited the ruins of the great Buddhist temple, where quite recently were discovered a few bones of the holy man in a copper box. You will have perhaps noticed a good deal about it in the papers of late. Both are some 1,800 years old. It was most interesting to go over the whole place with the man who found both temple and bones, one Dr. Spooner, an American.

Yesterday was a red-letter day. We went through the Kyber Pass right up to the frontier of Afghanistan. The frontier is a little unsettled, so Roos-Keppel had the road guarded by Kyber Rifles. The *partie carrée* consisted of the Chief Commissioner, the Hon. Maurice Wingfield, and his clever, good-looking wife, and myself. We started in a motor at 8 a.m., getting back about dusk. It is not very safe to be out after dark. We went right up to the frontier of Afghanistan. We rode a pony up a break-neck path to the Pishgar Ridge and looked towards Afghanistan along the Cabul road. The view is very impressive and extraordinarily wild. We then returned to Lundi Kotal Fort, the headquarters of the Kyber Rifles, a fine regiment of Afridis commanded by picked officers of the Indian Army. A charming set of men, clear-eyed, keen, smart, intelligent, and modest. I was much struck by them. Their life is daily in their hands. On the way back we passed the fort of Ali Masjid placed on the top of an almost unclimbable rock, and later on Jamrood Fort, the last before reaching Peshawar. The old frontier men like Lord Lawrence were quite right. Their policy was quite sound. We should leave Afghanistan severely alone. If any mistake has been made, it is probably that we have advanced too far. I cannot see that it matters two straws whether we go up to one ridge or another. We hold the Kyber and that is all that can matter, and as for a Russian advance into India, well, I should say, "Come and see the country." Some of the tribes are cut-throat robbers, and all we need do is to keep them in check. They are fairly in hand. No doubt they are now more or less well armed, but it is quite likely that they will, if carefully watched, but not interfered with, settle down. Peshawar is wonderfully well kept, and is clean, tidy, and picturesque. Some of the people seem to pass their time either cutting each other's throats or catching each other's pigeons. The city is surrounded by high walls and has sixteen gates. The Bala Hissar Fort, built by General Avitabile, an Italian, is fine, and from the top the view is superb. The said General used to hang three citizens a day just to encourage the rest. I am excessively glad I came. The whole of this frontier is extremely interesting, and the people are a fine, manly, cut-throat-looking set. But it is hard work this life I lead, and I feel a good bit "tucked up," as the saying is.

The great event of my visit was a reception of all the native nobles. And all for "poor little me"! I have already had to go through a native concert in my honour. Oh, misery! The reception was the most picturesque sight I ever saw in a civilised house. Every kind of man dressed in every kind of garb. From the pleader (lawyer) in English dress-clothes, to Pathan, Afridi, and every other tribal nobility in their everyday national clothes. Some huge men amongst them. One was six feet seven. They are absolutely natural and "care nothink for nobbody." They began to arrive at 9 and stopped till 11—evening. They filed past and chatted with me in strange tongues, and were regaled on small plates filled with sweets and cakes. The Hindoos (they are only a few here) had their "spread" apart and drank wine, which the others do not touch. They all seem a fine, manly, independent lot of people. Before the party I went to look at the museum. More Buddha relics, and sundry objects of interest. My second expedition has been most interesting, but not quite so successful. On November 2nd we started at 6 a.m. and went to Nowshera Cantonment. It is the home of a good strong force and is well placed. We did not stop there but went on to the Cavalry Camp, where we breakfasted with General Angelo and his newly married, very attractive Australian wife. Then we went on to Mardan, the headquarters of the Guides, who have their mess in a really beautiful plantation. Eventually we reached Dargai Fort (52nd Sikhs) at the foot of the frontier mountains. There the climb began. Solid miles of corkscrew road through the pass into the Swat Valley. We reached the Malakand Fort at last and lunched with the Political Officer, who lives in a small house perched up on the hill-top, where the leopards literally come in to tea. The view towards Chitral over the valley of the Swat River is fine and striking. Again I was impressed by the absurdity of the Russian invasion scare. Personally I much doubt if the Russians ever meant to work into India. They probably meant to keep us occupied while they did as they pleased in Central Asia and Persia. Be that as it may, their advance on India now is an absurdity. The Swat tribes seem quiet and the valley is very fertile. The whole thing was to me intensely interesting. We broke down half-way down the mountain and I thought we were "done," but I managed to get hold of an Army transport cart with a couple of aged mules and a native driver, and we crawled down to Nowshera, where the Guides gave us a kindly welcome and refreshing tea. We left at 6, but when we got about thirty miles on we had a second bad break-down, and Sir George refused to take us farther, as he contended that there is risk on the road at night. We struck the railway more by luck than good management, and found a helpful station-master at a small station. He rigged up a trolly, got a lamp and some coolies, and we ran along the line of rails in the middle of the night through a tree-darkened country, with birds and beasts startled out of their poor lives. It was not easy to hold on, and I was so tired I nearly fell off from sheer sleep more than once. We reached Nowshera at midnight and managed to get some food. We had lunched at 12.30 and had tea at 4, so that we were starving. At Nowshera we had to wait till 4 a.m. for the Bombay mail, and we did not get home till 7. Twenty-five hours' continuous travelling—train, horses, transport mule-cart, trolly, train, and carriage. We were simply dead beat, but I have now seen Northern India and the two frontiers, and that I most wanted to do.

From Peshawar I went to Nahan, in Sirmoor State. More strenuous life! I left Roos-Keppel's hospitable house at dewy morn on the 3rd instant, reaching Barara Station at 6 a.m. on the 5th—that is to say, my shattered remains reached that said station. There I procured a tonga, which is a bone-breaking, two-wheeled "machine" with a pair of spavined and otherwise unhealthy horses, and two *ekkas*, which are ditto with one wretched pony. I loaded up my luggage, rifles, jemadar (a man with a sword—man and sword equally useless), and bearer—*i.e.*, valet. We did thirty miles in a scorching sun and in clouds of red dust. Then I got on a prancing charger and rode up the mountain, sick with terror at having to leave my luggage and, above all, my beloved rifles. I was met by General Bier Bikram Singh near the gates of Nahan, the capital of Sirmoor, and deafened by salutes going off in my honour. I was very tired, having ridden fourteen miles in a saddle the size of a postage stamp. I then had to pay my respects to the Maharajah, and attended a tennis match of the two young Princes. At last I retired to the "Guest-house," where I was gorgeously housed and attended to by numerous retainers. I had an excellent dinner alone. Next day I reviewed the Sirmoor Imperial Troops, called on officials, visited the foundry, and generally saw sights with polite resignation. On Sunday I went into camp to shoot anything that came. There is but little game to be had, and yet only fifty years ago wild beasts rendered it wellnigh a risk to get here at all. I believe there are any number of panthers, but they are very cunning and rarely get shot. I hate reviews, but, sleepy as I was, I had to turn out at 6 to review the Imperial Service Contingent, commanded by General Bier Bikram Singh. He is a very keen soldier, is a Colonel in the English Army, and has fought for us in two expeditions. The troops, about 500 men, are quite marvellous. I have seen the

Guards march past no better at home. There was a smart cavalry troop and a perfectly appointed two-gun battery and some 500 infantry. One cannot take up an illustrated paper without seeing a picture of the Secretary of State in a top-hat "taking the salute" at home, so I suppose I may be forgiven for doing so on the top of an Indian mountain. But I felt a horrible fraud on a huge grey horse from Cabul and in a military saddle into the bargain. Because I had been in South Africa they were persuaded that I am habitually up to my neck in blood. I also did the hospital, the barracks and all the rest, and am quite done myself.

I was enchanted with Nahan (pronounced Narn). It is beautifully situate on the top of a mountain with glorious views from every side. It is exquisitely clean, as tidy as possible, the buildings in perfect repair, and the people are happy, bright, and prosperous. Even the animals seem well cared for. Simla is quite squalid compared to Nahan, and what I like is that there is not a European in the latter place except the manager of the foundry. Both the Maharajah and his brother are capable, kind, enlightened men and an example to many Englishmen. I am very glad to have been to Sirmoor, as it is a revelation and an education. It shows what intelligent, well-bred Indian rulers can do if we do not interfere with them. The foundry is an instance of intelligent enterprise. It was started by the late Maharajah and seems to be a success financially. But it is a hot job going over a foundry in India! And I have seen so many in England. I was also honoured by a gymkhana. I hate sports as much as reviews. Why anyone should wish to put a ball in a particular hole, or why a rational human being should wish to get to the top of a greasy pole, I never could understand; but sports in India are worth seeing on account of the bright sun, the brilliant colours, the graceful race, and the picturesque surroundings. After the usual tent-pegging, etc., we had a grand sham-fight, which was extraordinarily funny. The Indians are born actors, and the " wounded " in their agony contortions were too comical for words, as was the imitation of English officers. The sports wound up with a torchlight musical ride, one of the most effective rides I have ever seen. I had to give away the prizes and make an oration, and crawled on to a sofa after standing from 3.30 till 7. The start for the shooting camp was at 5 a.m., and I could hardly see I was so tired. The camp was pitched in a beautiful spot by a swift, clear river, and the forest was a real forest of deciduous trees just turning gold and red. But it was in a fever-stricken spot, and down I went in two hours. I dared not disappoint my host, who had gone to much trouble and expense, but the misery of jolting all day on an elephant when one is racked by fever is beyond words. We saw no game. Here also all seemed shot off. I was really glad of it, for I could not have lifted my rifle. I crawled into bed after two cups of boiling tea and much aspirin, and shook till 1 a.m., when I got to sleep. The second day I shot two wild-boar, the third day a small-headed but large-bodied sambhar stag, but on the fourth day I got a beauty, a huge stag. The head is a very good one, and that is what I wanted. On November 11th I regretfully left Nahan and travelled for nine solid hours, leaving at daybreak—four hours on horse-back and the rest in a horrible tonga. The heavy work—*i.e.*, crossing rivers, climbing pathless mountains, and travelling along nullahs or dry water-courses—we did on elephants; the rest on foot or in the saddle. My elephant's name was "Mr. Wellskin." He had a bad reputation for temper. His worst trick was picking up a stone with his trunk and smashing the head of any casual passer-by with it, but I fed him on apples and biscuits and we became quite fast friends. I failed to get a leopard although they were round the camp every night and carried off an unfortunate dog, also a poor goat. I suppose I shall get one in due course.

At Lucknow I stopped long enough to call on the Hewetts. I devoted some time to the ruined Residency and the Baillie Gate and Guard-house. I am glad to have stood by the grave of Henry Lawrence, "who tried to do his duty," and in the room in which he died. The ruined Residency and the Baillie Gate and Guardroom are most im-pressive, and it interested me greatly to go down into the cellar where Nancy Brown fancied she heard the bagpipes of the relieving Highlanders. The graveyard is very interesting, and I was sorry not to be able to devote more time to it. I have a relation buried there who got the Victoria Cross when a Light Dragoon subaltern. He was killed at twenty-one.

From Lucknow I went to Benares. The Maharajah is a clever, friendly man, who showed me much kindness. He lent me his carriage and I went the round of the temples. One of them, the monkey temple, is full of monkeys who expect to be fed. They are quite tame. The golden temple has a gilt dome, hence its name; but they are all rather poor compared to some of the Mahomedan mosques. Benares is the home of flies, mosquitoes, and beggars, but it is none the less very attractive. I reached Gya on the 15th. There is only one thing worth seeing there, and that is the great Buddhist temple, which entails a seven miles' drive. I have now seen most of the best Mahomedan, Hindoo, and Buddhist temples, and wild horses will not drag me to see another.

I got to Calcutta on the 16th and have taken up my quarters at 15, Kyd Street, where I shall be a fixture with incessant work and worry till April. I have the pleasure of paying a fortune for a house which in London would be dear at a third of the rent. India is no longer the country to save money in.

I have already seen a cobra killed in the garden.

LETTER VII.—SUNDERBUNDS AND BUFFALO

CALCUTTA, *January 6th*, 1910.

BY sheer hard labour I was "well on time," as Americans say, with my work; in fact, I was ahead of my department, so my merciful staff allowed me to take a week off for Christmas, and I went to my beloved Sunderbunds in a launch which I had lent me. I did not expect to get any shooting, but I took my rifles on the chance. The journey to Khulna from Calcutta is detestable, as one arrives at 4 a.m.—an unholy time to turn out and a feverish time of day to start on a steamer. The sunrise was superb, and the river, fringed with palms, backed by alternations of paddy-fields and dense bamboo jungles, suddenly lighted up to a golden red, was a delight to gaze on. The sunrise seemed to respond to the Vedic hymn:

> "Bright luminous dawn: rose-red, radiant, rejoicing!
> Open the gates of the morning: waken the singing birds!"*

Paddy, I may mention, is rice. But the air was cold and damp and laden with miasma. Unlike the Hooghly, this river, the Barisal, is full of bird life. Vultures, kites, ospreys, cranes, and all kinds of sea and fresh-water fowl; and at intervals one may see crocodiles basking in the sun or sleep-

* Steele.

ing at the water-edge. Porpoises dart gracefully across the steamer's bow, and half-wild cattle come down to bathe and drink. It is a delightful trip and quite to my taste, as it is altogether Indian.

The steamer stops at intervals to land and take up natives, and the process is well worth watching. A gondola-like boat with a free-board of about 2 inches is crammed with Indians who stand on a few rough planks, packed like sardines. That they do not go overboard always surprises me. Occasionally they do, and then results a slump in baboos and a tidy meal for Mr. Crocodile. I know nothing more delightful than this river trip. It *obliges* one to forget Calcutta and Simla. It is the India of John Company's time. Just at this time of year the river is full of craft. The boats are most wonderful native creations and they all have different coloured sails—pink, red, green, heliotrope, yellow, brown, and white. They are very picturesque and a delight to the eye. They bring rice, jute, and millet to Barisal, whence it is taken to Calcutta in large steam-floats.

At Barisal I found my friend Herman Meyer. I called on his wife, a nice, cheery, bright-eyed lady and very young-looking to be the mother of three half-grown-up sons.

Meyer and I started for the Bay of Bengal in a cranky fifty-year-old launch with a marvellous Indian-built engine warranted to give in at short notice. Our destination was the island of Mookeri in the open sea. Our launch drew only 2½ feet of water and is a river boat, so we ran a risk in taking her out to sea. But a rumour had reached Meyer that on the island, which is uninhabited, there dwelt a herd of prehistoric buffalo. We reached the island on Tuesday morning at daybreak (December 21st). To our intense delight, we made out with our glasses some buffalo near the shore.

We did not wait for breakfast, but rowed to shore at once. The island, like ancient Gaul, is divided into three parts: first there is a broad strip of sand; then a strip of marsh land covered with short grass and about a mile wide; inside this belt is a dense jungle of stunted, small trees. We made straight for the jungle and soon saw a large herd of buffalo cows and calves grazing on the grass belt. I think they were four small herds bunched together. We walked, or rather crept, cautiously up to them, but saw no bulls. Later on we made out four bulls grazing apart about 300 yards from us, and some 100 yards separating the one from the other. We decided to get up two trees and send the boat close inshore with a shot-gun, hoping the firing would scare the bulls and drive them to the jungle. But buffalo are the least timid and the most savage brutes existing. All they did was to walk to the water-edge, stamp and snort, and look savagely at the boat. No native will willingly beat up buffalo. We dared not stop in the Bay of Bengal at night, especially as it looked like rough weather. I was "mad keen" to get a buffalo, and in spite of Meyer's protest, I determined to stalk the bulls and shoot. I crept to within 200 yards, took a steady shot at the nearest, and knocked him over; then I knocked over a second one. Then I loaded, fired, and hit the other two. One moved slowly away, joined the stampeded herd, and I lost him, although I knew he was mortally wounded. The other wounded one at once attacked the two dying ones and gored their bodies, and then stood sentry over them. I waited some time in hopes he would move off, but he kept on walking from one to the other and refused to go away. The tide was beginning to turn and I knew we should have to leave the island in a short time. Meyer implored me to come away. I realised the folly of approaching a furious wounded buffalo, but I also knew that unless I shot him I should lose my trophies. I thought the matter well over and I deliberately elected to risk it. I walked up to within 100 yards of the buffalo, fired, and dropped him on his knees. He sprang up again at once and charged me at a fearful pace. I stood quite still and fired at the nape of his neck. I fired too low and hit him in the face. Then I knew I was done for. I had no second rifle, and I had hardly time to think. All I could do and did was to stand still, turn sideways, and try to avoid the points of the horns. In this I succeeded, but the buffalo caught me on the right thigh and tossed me 10 feet in the air, right over his back. Meyer says I turned a complete somersault in the air with my rifle in my hand, and came down right on the top of my head. I landed in mud and sent up a small column of mud and water. The buffalo turned to finish me, but in so doing he caught sight of a flying native, one of our men, whose loin-cloth was flapping in the wind, and which no doubt caught the buffalo's eye. He raced after the poor man, overtook him, and drove his horn, low down, into his back. I thought my thigh was broken, as I could not rise, so I just lay still in the mud and looked on. My rifle was choked with mud and I could not open it; besides, my eyes, nose, ears, and mouth were literally full of mud and I was terribly shaken. It was a horrible sight. The bull rushed about with his tail in the air, roaring and carrying the wretched man upright on his horns.

Presently he caught sight of Meyer's rifle carrier, who had bolted, leaving Meyer without cartridges, raced after him and tossed him, but did him no great harm. Then he came back to finish me, but Meyer most pluckily approached and fired at him, and his and my previous shots told; blood was pouring from his nostrils, and after getting to within a few yards of me, he lay down and died. With the help of some men I managed to crawl to the boat and was lifted on board the launch. I understand I am one of the very, very few men who have been tossed by a wild buffalo and lived to tell the tale. I took two large cups of boiling tea and was lifted into bed. I had a cruel night. The muscles of my back and neck were badly strained, I was bruised all over and a good bit shaken. Periostitis set in in my thigh, and I was in very acute pain for twelve hours. Hot fomentations and Elliman did me a world of good, and in the morning I crept on deck and lay in the sun looking at the three buffalo heads. "Three buffalo in thirty minutes," said I to myself, "are worth a tossing." I don't think I am seriously hurt. I shall be Röntgen-rayed to make sure the thigh-bone is not injured, and I shall enjoy looking at the head of the gentleman who tossed me. Some consolation for a man in his sixtieth year; but never again shall I walk up buffalo.

The poor wounded man suffered terribly. I doubt his recovering, although he is doing well, and as ill-luck would have it, we ran on to a sand-bank and had to remain on it for twelve hours till the tide turned. The sensation of being tossed is quite the most curious I ever experienced. One seems literally to fly through the air. But for the mud, I must have broken my neck. My sun-helmet was flattened and my neck is as stiff as if I had been half hanged. While on the sand-bank we had only 1 foot of water, and the sailors and servants walked about round the launch, which fortunately, being a paddle-boat, lay on an even keel, and eventually floated on a flood-tide quite uninjured. We had to anchor in a *karl*, where I hired a native sailing-boat on to which we shipped the injured man and sent him straight to Barisal Hospital. The native boat could go by a shallower channel and could beat the launch by a day.

Whilst we were getting the launch shipshape off Gurli Char Island, preparatory to starting on our return journey, the local landlord came on board and begged us to land and shoot a tiger which had mauled a man and was killing their cattle. Do you remember the picture of the terrier—"Who said rats ?" I was just like that terrier—"Who said tiger ?" Meyer protested that he had had quite enough of taking me after big game, and declared he would not be at rest till he had put me into the train and ceased to be answerable for me, but he is a keen sportsman and the kindest of men, and my coaxing and obstinacy prevailed, and we tied up "kills" that evening. On Boxing Day we sallied forth. I will not dwell on my feelings, in the literal sense of the word, whilst being helped into and out of the jolly-boat. I could not, if I wished, do justice to them during the hobble of nearly a mile of alternate lumps of wet and sun-baked mud, and the less said the better in regard to the process of getting me on to a tree-fork. When at last I settled down like a crow with a broken wing, I found that I could shoot on all sides but one. Said I to myself, "If there be a tiger, he will of course come where I cannot shoot him"—and he did. I knew I could not stand the jar of a heavy rifle, so I had taken my light paradox gun which shoots a hollow-nosed bullet. The tiger only showed me his flank for a second and I had to shoot from my left shoulder, a feat I do not profess to be able to perform successfully. I smashed his thigh and then hit him somewhere in the body with the second barrel. He roared like a bull and fell flat down in the jungle grass, but just managed to get away. The jungle grass was very thick and several feet high. I am afraid I shall never get him, although he is no doubt dead. We had to steam off at daybreak next morning, and all we could do was to leave two good shikaris on the island promising them a handsome reward if they turned up in Calcutta with the skin. They may; but it is not likely, as they will not face a wounded tiger, and small blame to them. On the other hand, if the tiger is dead, he will be curled up in some very thick patch of jungle and will in due course be eaten by jackals, rats, and vultures.

I am terribly disappointed. He was a grand tiger, and I did all I possibly could. It is a wonder I hit him at all, as I was too stiff to turn, and rifle-shooting from the left shoulder is extraordinarily difficult. I would give anything to have got that tiger.

I do not suppose the performance did my leg any good, but unless a man is willing to take risks, and at times big ones, it is not a bit of use his attempting to shoot big game. Of course, in the case of princely personalities such as Viceroys and Governors, the risk is reduced to vanishing-point and discomfort to non-existence; but if one wants to shoot big game in real sporting fashion, both risk and discomfort have to be faced, and that is the long and short of it. I do it deliberately and enjoy it, although I am much too old. In India very few men go on shooting big game after fifty, except on elephants, and they are wise in their generation. I have had to begin at fifty-nine, and am greatly handicapped in consequence, but I "just love it," as women say.

I was tossed on the 21st and, Meyer was very anxious to get me to a doctor, but I felt sure rest and quiet were all I required, and nowhere could I get that better than on the launch, so we anchored in a lovely bay formed by three islands—ideal isles: palms, pampas-grass and peepul-trees, a glorious sun and a fresh, healthy breeze. We remained there till after Christmas Day. The

Serang (or Captain) had shot a bar-necked goose, off which we dined, finishing up with marrow-bone. Not even the Travellers' Club could produce such a marrow-bone. To most men a marrow-bone is a marrow-bone, "and it is nothing more." But that one meant much more to me, for it had belonged to the buffalo who tossed me. I *did* enjoy that marrow-bone! I also enjoyed looking at the three sets of horns, to which I shall, I hope, add the fourth, for I promised some fishermen a hatful of rupees if they found and sent me the fourth head. The buffalo could not live many hours and the vultures will indicate where he lies. The heads are very fair ones; one, indeed, is quite a good one. They are worth a toss: *Paris vaut bien une messe*, as Henry of Navarre said when reproached with becoming a Holy Roman. I lay on deck in the sun all day and dozed, and the absolute rest, silence, and absence of all worry did me a world of good, and I am really nearly myself again. Of course, I shall be lame for a bit and unable to ride, but I can already hobble about with a stick, and my leg looks like a leg—which it certainly did not for some days. It is still a fine purple-brown from my hip to my ankle, and painful, but no lasting harm is done, I hope.

We reached Barisal on the 27th, Calcutta on the 28th, and on the 29th I resumed work. Till April I shall be up to my eyes in work; worry, and vexation.

Nothing could have exceeded Meyer's coolness, pluck, and devotion from first to last.

The damage is a go of pleurisy from a crushed rib, a jarred thigh-bone, and water on the knee;

but as I am quite young I shall soon get over it all!

It is difficult to write about sport without appearing to sing a hymn of self-praise. To show that I am conscious of my own (as well as other folks') infirmities, I quote from an Indian paper the following note, appending a confession of my own depravity:

A Sportsman's Qualities.

"Now, the indispensable qualifications of a good shot are sureness of eye, steadiness of nerve and hand, cool and prompt decision. Without these a man may be a sportsman, but he can never be an expert shot. He could never face with equal mind the tiger or the buffalo, or even the pheasant and the snipe. Sureness of eye and steadiness of nerve and hand may be gifts of nature, but like all such gifts they require care and cultivation. No qualities of the body and mind are more sensitive to the conditions of a man's life; none deteriorate more rapidly from abuse, none respond more readily to self-control. To remain a good shot after forty is the best testimony any man can produce of temperance in all things, of a life so well ordered that its powers and perceptions are unimpaired."

I humbly admit that I am a living testimony to the opposite. Never have I been able to do anything temperately; but I can still shoot, and for "after forty" you may read "after sixty."

LETTER VIII.—REFORMED LEGISLATIVE COUNCIL, 1910

CALCUTTA, *January 25th*, 1910.

On this eventful day the "elected of the people" (not a large crowd), the "selected of the Viceroy," and the "guilded of the Civil Service," in other words the Reformed Legislative Council, met for the first time in the transmogrified council chamber in Calcutta. Lazarus and Co., the upholsterers, have made an excellent job of the room. Two galleries, one for the Press and one for the public, add to the accommodation but detract from the ventilation. The Viceroy's chair has been raised some 18 inches, and the old long table has been replaced by a new short one. Warren Hastings retains his place (and his cold, cynical smile), but is rather more skyed, and the other portraits remain as they were—Lords Cornwallis and Minto (1807) on one side and Lords Teignmouth and Wellesley on the other.

The members were almost all present, and the *coup d'œil*, thanks to the different dresses and colours, was picturesque. The swearing in was interesting, as so many religions were represented, and the form of taking the oath was varied and in some cases peculiar. The public, mainly "sassiety" ladies, clapped timidly when His

Excellency finished his oration, but the Council itself looked, and no doubt felt, too frightened to give any *signe de vie*.

Having listened to Lord Minto's brave words and been duly impressed thereby, we walked solemnly out, and thus ended the first sitting of the Reformed Council.

LETTER IX.—LEGISLATIVE COUNCIL DINNER

CALCUTTA, *February 16th*, 1910.

I INITIATED yesterday evening, to the great detriment of my bank balance, an entirely novel form of entertainment. I gave a dinner to all the members of the Reformed Legislative Council. We dined in the guests' room at the Bengal Club, and I question whether such a representative collection of Indians ever before met together at dinner. Some who, owing to caste, could not partake of food with me, came in after dinner. One, a charming man, dined (at a small separate table) on a huge mound of ice-cream and some very indigestible plum-cake, and drank much iced water—he still lives. Some were vegetarians, many were teetotallers and non-smokers. On the other hand, not a few ate like troopers and drank wine freely, which, however, must not be taken to mean that any of them took more than they could carry.

I thought well to break up the party into sets of five and seat them at separate small tables, and so avoid as much as possible all difficulties about rank and precedence—a terribly "rocky" question in India.

At my table I had Burdwan, Mamudahbad,

Ranbir Sing of Patiala, and Nawab Saiyid Muhammad of Madras.

They all came in ordinary evening-dress, except one, who wore a really beautiful dress of dove-coloured satin, embroidered with gold. Patiala and many others, of course, wore turbans, and one guest wore a black astrakhan cap. The excellent cut and fit of the dress-clothes worn by Indian gentlemen is very noticeable. Their dress-clothes are frequently better in all respects than those of the average Anglo-Indians, myself included. The only jarring note at the dinner in regard to dress was the large butterfly *yellow* tie of a European guest. Although I was the host, I may be permitted to say that the Bengal Club provided a very good dinner, and the wines were excellent.

The whole thing went off remarkably well, and I was much gratified by the cordiality and good-fellowship which prevailed. The bright and intelligent conversation, which never flagged, and the cheery good-humoured expression on every-one's face, led me to hope that my object had been attained—viz., the establishment of a feeling of *bonne camaraderie* between the many, very dissimilar, representatives of the first approach to Indian elective constituencies and the Indian Civilian nominees of the Provincial Governments.

I should find it difficult in London, or indeed in any European capital, to get together a set of men more intelligent, more interesting, and of more refined manners than the Indians who dined with me on February 15th, 1910, at the Bengal Club in Calcutta.

What led to the dinner was this:

The Reformed Legislative Council is the chief feature of the Morley reforms—reforms which may appear unduly circumscribed, but which are, I feel sure, destined to lead to far-reaching changes in the future, and, as I think, changes for the better.

The old dispensation answered well enough in the past. Our rule has been beneficent, and above all a just one, but it is unsuited to present-day conditions. We have given Indians not only Western education, we have given them Western ideals, and it is idle to suppose that a mild despotism can remain acceptable to the India of the twentieth century. A recognition of this fact has come none too soon. A genuine participation in the government of their own country with a view to eventual self-government is but a natural sequence to the educational development which we have ourselves introduced, and the Indians are quite obviously entitled to political reform. I realised shortly after its first meeting that the Reformed Council into which the elected element has been introduced would not work smoothly unless something were done to weld it into a homogeneous gathering. Being an Englishman, a dinner at once suggested itself to my mind as a simple method by which sharp corners could be rounded and rough edges smoothed. Accordingly I decided on asking the whole of the members to dinner.

The few friends, official and otherwise, whom I consulted threw the coldest of cold water on the proposal. IThe ndians would resent it—Mahomedans would object to dine with Hindoos and *vice versa*—high caste and low caste would decline to meet—Europeans would keep away—I did not know India—this sort of thing would not do—and so forth. The Viceroy tried to dissuade me from attempting the impossible, and I was even told that it would be "very unfair" to ask such different elements to sit down to dinner together.

When I sounded the members individually, however, I found certainly some surprise but ready acquiescence.

The Bengal Club very courteously allowed me the use of their Guest Banqueting Hall (I had anticipated difficulty in this particular), and I issued my invitations. The response was general, warm and appreciative, and the result proved that you have only to get Indians and Indians and English and Indians to rub shoulders unofficially to obtain a very happy result.

LETTER X.—REFORMED COUNCIL SESSION, 1910

CALCUTTA, *April*, 1910.

THE first Session of the Reformed Council has come to an end, and it has been a living testimony to the wisdom and foresight of Lord Morley, for his reform has worked well and advantageously. But it is a legislative revolution which has thrown a very, very heavy burden on the Finance Minister—a burden which will increase until it becomes unbearable unless a change is made in one respect.

The present procedure admits of every conceivable subject being discussed during the Budget debate, and of this very full advantage is naturally taken. In fact, the debate assumes the character of a debate on the adjournment in the House of Commons, and the unfortunate Finance Minister has little or no rest during the greater part of the Session.

I find that my remarks cover no less than 73 foolscap pages of print (and Heaven knows I have every desire to keep silence), and the whole debate on Finance represents no less than 376 pages of close print.

By a curious coincidence the presentation of my first Budget synchronised, as to the month, with one introduced exactly half a century ago by my namesake the Rt. Hon. James Wilson. His was, I believe, the first Financial Statement presented in India. It covered just one sheet of paper and the figures in support seven.

The revenue he estimated at 38 millions as against 74 now, and the expenditure at 42 as against 73½ now.

The total imports and exports amounted to 60 million as against 200 of this year.

There is a curious parallelism between his speech and mine. He had to deal with a deficit, he had to convey a grave warning (which was long unheeded) of the precarious nature of our opium revenue, and he had to suggest additional taxation.

That is precisely what I have had to do this Session.

The impression I have received from the general trend and tone of the debates is that Indian members realise to the full the responsibility they have acquired, and that they will work the reform with credit to themselves and advantage to their country.

I have impressed on the Indian members that it is rather by the painstaking examination of specific items of expenditure than by framing abstract resolutions on organic changes in financial policy that economy can best be attained. Also that advantageous services can be more readily provided by means of savings effected than by appeals for additional funds, which the finances of the country cannot produce without casting additional burdens on the people.

They do not in the least resent my attitude and seem rather to welcome a professorial address.

They are terribly in earnest and devour with avidity any remarks illustrative of the House of Commons methods, for a Parliament is their ideal, a Parliament they mean, *à la longue*, to get, and a Parliament in the end they will possess; always assuming that British India remains British India.

It is early days for me to formulate even a purely private opinion, but I have already learnt that as a general rule the most unreliable opinion is that of men who have passed most of their lives in India. They seem unable to appreciate to their full extent the vital, incessant, and very rapid changes which are taking place in India. The early impressions they received appear to dominate their views.

In British India there has been up to now a slow period of evolution; from Wellesley's small supreme Council to the Charter Act of 1833, followed by the Charter Act of 1853, to the Council Acts of 1861 and 1892, up to the Act of 1909 constituting the present "Reformed Council."

We shall have to face a great acceleration in the future. "The growth of Education is bearing fruit. Important classes of the population are learning to realise their own position, to estimate for themselves their own intellectual capacities, and to compare their claims for an equality of citizenship with those of a ruling race" (Minto).

The present reforms have not opened the flood-gates, but they have let out a fairly strong flow of water, and more will force its way through.

Torn asunder from all my Western interests; the Indian problem has become an obsession. It is ever present all day and every day and, alas! many nights.

I can see but two solutions in the future—either complete self-government or the breaking up of British India into Native States with the retention of a large enclave in each presidency, the whole under a member of the Royal Family as Vice-Emperor.

The latter alternative strikes one as a startling proposition, but is the alternative none the less. It would be quite impossible to maintain the present practically autocratic rule of a Viceroy and at the same time give India self-government. The Viceroyalty would have to become a headship and no more in either case.

The attachment of all Indians to our Royal Family is traditional and touchingly genuine. A "royal" Vice-Emperor would be more than welcome in India. He would become an invaluable asset to us and a treasured possession to Indians.

In allusion to European unrest the remark has often been made to me by educated Indians of every class: "If there is trouble in England, tell the King-Emperor to come to India, where he shall be a loved and powerful Sovereign."

The exaggeratedly high standard of efficiency which we have set up would no doubt become somewhat attenuated under either alternative, but it is quite an open question whether we are not imposing on India a standard of efficiency in excess of her actual requirements.

In any case the human equation is a factor which cannot be ignored, and it is but human to prefer reasonably good government administered by one's own race rather than extreme efficiency at the hands of an alien race.

At the risk of seeming presumptuous, I add that, whilst the English race is absolutely the first in the creation of a Colony, it inclines to ignore that the child has grown up. It insists on imposing its own constitution, its own political methods, and its own none too perfect administration on communities, races, and creeds however unsuitable they may be.

It might become a question whether Native State Government may not prove more suitable than any other. Certainly the condition of Mysore, Travancore, and Hyderabad, for instance, seems to indicate that prosperity and contentment are quite compatible with the rule of Indian Princes.

Undoubtedly British India is not yet ripe for self-government, but if all goes well it very soon will be, and if British India is to continue, prudent statesmanship will plough the self-government furrow and put the seed into it.

The one thing to be avoided is the imposition on India of a purely Western organisation unsuited to Eastern habits, instincts, and prejudices.

LETTER XI.—SAMBHALPUR—BISON NEPAL

SIMLA, *May 19th*, 1910.

MY spring tour has been a broken one. I left Calcutta on April 1st immediately after the Budget was passed, and went to Sambhalpur for a week. I had to return to Calcutta for some official and business interviews, and could not make a long stay in the Mufassal. On arrival at Sambhalpur I drove to a camp which my friend Moberly had established some thirty miles out, and there met for the first time his wife, an attractive and most companionable woman. I should think she must be an ideal Mufassal wife, for she managed everything admirably on a perfectly comfortable but economical basis and was never at a loss nor out of temper. My knee was too painful and water-logged to admit of any walking, and I had little, if any, hope of being able to do any shooting. In the evening Moberly casually mentioned that "a very unusual thing had occurred: a small herd of bison had appeared in this neighbourhood." Now, what I want particularly to do (but see but little chance of doing) is to shoot a bison. First of all there are not many left, secondly they are very shy, and thirdly the only way to get them is to stalk them on foot, sometimes for several days continuously.

As I could not walk 10 yards, I saw but little prospect of realising my desire. Moberly was much adverse to my attempting it, quite rightly insisting that it was 100 to 1 on my inflaming my knee and 100 to 1 against my getting anywhere near a bison. But my entreaties and his excessive good-nature combined resulted in the maddest wild-goose chase after bison the shikar world has ever seen. The Dewan of Patna State, a good friend of mine, had sent his pony some fifty miles across country and placed it at my disposal. The little chap stood about 12 hands and clearly resented carrying 12 stone. He did it for two days and then expressed his feelings by curling up suddenly like a collapsible toy and refusing to carry me any farther. I thought the mad chase was perforce ended, but the resourceful Mrs. Moberly at once produced, and insisted on my using, her dandy, which is a sort of chair slung between two poles. In this I continued the pursuit till it became difficult to turn in the jungle; so finally I transferred my aching bones to a charpoi, or native bed, and so devotedly did my beloved jungli men work that we never lost touch with the bison, and the junglis actually performed the extraordinary feat of working me up to within 500 yards of the bull. Those who know the extreme difficulty of stalking bison in saal woods over crackling dry leaves will agree that it was a wonderful performance. I believe I should have got that bull, but, alas! a traveller (unknown to us; and himself unconscious of intrusion) crossed the jungle between us and the bison, and the bull, like De Wet, stampeded through the line, and with his four wives and one son was seen no more. I never saw him at all. It was cruel ill-luck, but I felt almost more sorry for Moberly and the devoted jungli folk than I did for myself, and that is saying a great deal. The heat throughout was very severe, and the air was laden with hot ashes from the forest fires, which have been very prevalent this season.

I returned to Calcutta a sadder, a sorer, but a keener shikari than ever. But I shall never shoot a bison. I am past the stalking age; besides, stalking in bed is hardly a likely way of getting up to bison! Disappointment-week number one.

Early in the winter I received an offer to organise, and to manage for me, a shoot in Nepal. I asked Sir Chandra Sham Shere Jung, Prime Minister of Nepal, to be so kind as to grant me a permit to shoot at the foot of the Nepalese Himalaya Mountains. The Nepal Government were kindness itself, not only granting me a permit, but altering the dates and the locality twice to suit my convenience.

All through the winter and during my heavy work I looked forward with the keenest pleasure to the trip to Nepal. The Nepalese or Gurkhas are a most interesting people for whom I feel great sympathy and regard.

I left Simla just at the end of April and found myself, after two days and a night's travelling by rail, motor, and elephant, on the banks of the Sardah River—a beautiful river, watering a magnificent grazing country, which in years gone by must have been very full of game of all sorts, but which has now become a valuable and fairly well populated grazing country.

6

I had taken the precaution to write that when I was on a shooting expedition my ambition was to be, not a member of the Government of India, but a plain shikari. I said that all I wanted was a very small tent, the plainest possible food, and that I never drank anything but a little weak brandy-and-water. I found a *bandobast* prepared consisting of thirty-three elephants, fourteen camels, and numberless bullock waggons of every sort and kind. The dining-tent would have done well for the presentation of prizes at athletic sports—one tent was big enough for six, and mine big enough for three. The whole thing made me feel very miserable and, I fear, excessively irritable; the food and drink arrangements might have been run by the Savoy.

The result of all this was that we frequently did not get our dinner till well into the night; that on more than one occasion we parted company with half our transport, and that it was impossible ever to start either early or even punctually.

One of our difficulties was everyone's entire ignorance of the localities in which we were supposed to shoot.

I think after this I need hardly add that we had very poor sport. What made it all especially annoying was that we were in close touch with tigers the whole time. I have little hesitation in saying that had I been alone, I should have brought back more than one tiger skin.

On the other hand, there were redeeming features about the expedition. The country to me was of immense interest. The people especially attracted me; but what appealed to me most—I may almost say what also pained me most—was the marked contrast between the condition of a country and of its inhabitants governed and administered by the Nepalese, and that of some parts of India which I have seen which are governed and administered by us. The contrast was, I regret to say, unfavourable to our rule. In Nepal the people look well nourished, well developed, bright, self-reliant, and happy. The villages are a picture of neatness, and I believe that every one contains a guest-room so scrupulously clean and so nicely kept that a European can with safety put his bedding on the floor and go to sleep on it. Their drinking-water is kept in well-covered and clean cisterns, which results in the inhabitants being very free, I am told, from the diseases so prevalent in India. The cattle might almost be English cattle; the herds are large and the beasts themselves are sleek and fat. The women are all dressed rather like Scottish labourers' wives of old days—they appear very well-to-do, having a great number of heavy silver necklets and bracelets. The men are well and powerfully built, and, so far as I can judge, extremely well disposed to any stranger who might come amongst them. The country generally presented a prosperous and a green appearance. The background of the Himalayas, wooded at the foot and bare higher up, and snow-capped in some cases, was very beautiful, and although the heat was intense, the air felt crisp and healthy, though I am informed that the whole district is very malarial. This is the only occasion on which I have taken quinine. I did so because I was assured that it was the height of imprudence to do without it, but I very much question whether I should have got fever even without quinine. The country is well watered, numerous streams feeding the Sardah River, and in one place I found what I have not seen except in Kashmir—a beautiful bubbling spring of drinkable water.

Tigers, I am quite certain, are plentiful in the district, but the methods adopted on the occasion of my visit precluded the possibility of getting one. I am inclined to think that they are mere cattle-lifters; their home is on the low wooded spurs of the Himalayas, and they only come down at night to kill and eat cattle and get back to their mountain fastnesses before daylight. It is only occasionally, I fancy, that a lazy, over-fed one lies up in the plains. One, and only one such, we came across. The poor brute was so gorged that he made no attempt to bolt, but tried to hide in a bog covered with reeds some 10 feet high and very dense. I have never taken part in shooting from a howdah before, and if the one occasion on which I saw a tiger so shot is a good specimen of what howdah-shooting means, I hope never to take part in it again. It was simply disgusting butchery. The unfortunate tiger was up to his belly in sticky mud, the small reed jungle in which he hid was completely surrounded by elephants, and every time the poor brute showed his nose, everyone fired two barrels at him. I am happy to say that his death cannot be laid at my door, as I did not fire. I saw the skin in camp, and it was more like a sieve than a tiger skin—*de gustibus non est disputandum*. I dare say shooting tigers from an elephant is very good sport; it does not appeal to me. I know many good men who enjoy shooting low pheasants; personally I prefer to miss high ones. Although I have a most kind invitation for next year from a charming Lieutenant-Governor of a province who is noted for his great shooting expeditions, I may not avail myself of it, because I care not for these royal progresses, which appear to me to be more suited to Fontainebleau than to the jungles of India.

For fifteen days we were hardly ever off an elephant's back; and I feel very tired and shaken, but on the whole, apart from the failure as regards sport, I have immensely enjoyed my outing, and am very glad indeed to have seen at any rate something of Nepal. I had never before been on friendly terms with elephants; I am not sure that I should ever care to trust them, but they are certainly interesting animal companions.

One sight I shall never forget—thirty-three huge elephants swimming in the Sardah River. On the back of each, which only showed about 2 inches above the water, stood a naked mahout, and the elephants themselves played about like a shoal of porpoises. Another very interesting sight is to see them having their bath. The mahouts make them lie down in very shallow water and wash them from head to foot just as a nurse washes a baby. It is curious to see these huge animals lifting up one leg and then another to have it well washed, blinking their eyes to prevent the water splashing into them, and generally behaving like naughty children who are determined to give the nurse who washes them as much trouble as possible. My own elephant, which rejoiced in the name of "Jasmine," was a magnificent female elephant, extraordinarily sagacious and marvellously staunch. The one tiger we saw got within a few inches of her trunk, but she merely curled it up and never stirred. She was so beautifully broken that if a deer or anything else got up while we were on the march, she of her own accord immediately stopped, so as to enable whoever was on her back to take a steady shot. I fed her plentifully on biscuits and by the time the trip was over we were fast friends.

With the exception of one or two heavy rain-storms and one severe hail-storm, the weather throughout was magnificent, and the heat, which most people would have found very trying, I found delightful. It tries my eyes, but with that exception, the hotter it is the better I feel. I returned to Simla on May 15th and was thankful to find that the bitter cold had been replaced by fine summer weather.

I am afraid my Nepal shooting trip must be set down as disappointment-week number two, as the only game I got was one very fine leopard measuring 7 feet 5 inches and an unusually good cheetal.

I shot the leopard under somewhat exceptional circumstances.

My attention was attracted to two wildly excited little birds, who fluttered and chattered angrily over a very small pond surrounded by reeds. I thought a snake was threatening their nest and got close to them. I then made out the head of the leopard lapping water. I shot him through the neck and killed him.

The little birds had been mobbing him.

LETTER XII.—BOMBAY AND "SERVANTS OF INDIA SOCIETY"

SIMLA, *September 2nd*, 1910.

I HAVE just returned from an official tour to the Bombay Presidency. I left Simla on August 15th and returned here on the 31st. Travelling through Central India was a great trial and the Bombay climate was at its worst. The heat in Alwar, Rewa, and Gwalior States, and also at Jhansi, was terrific. The whole thing has been rather too much of an undertaking for a man of my age, but I am very glad I went, as it was most important that I should get into touch with the financial, commercial, and industrial people of Bombay. I reached Bombay on the 17th, and on the 18th proceeded to Poona, where I was the guest of Sir George Clarke till Monday, the 22nd.

One of the most extraordinary features of Anglo-Indian life is the craving for incessant change of residence. The Governor of Bombay possesses no less than three official residences: one at Mahableshwar, which is a considerable journey from Bombay, where he passes some of the spring months; Ganeskhind, which is a small palace at Poona; and, of course, his official residence on Malabar Hill in Bombay. Ganeskhind is a most comfortable house of somewhat pretentious architecture, and enormous sums must in the past have been lavished upon it. The grounds are lovely, the gardens being the most interesting and the best kept in India, so far as my experience goes. It seemed to me that most of the shrubs and creepers, which are singularly beautiful, are either Cingalese or Japanese. The "compound," as it is called, is almost as large as a fair-sized English park and admits of a good game of golf being played in it. I was very much struck by the very tidy and well-kept look of the whole place, which I am afraid cannot be said of either the Calcutta or Simla palaces.

It is refreshing and educationally advantageous to talk over India with Sir George Clarke. He is a first-class man whose grasp of the situation, not only in his own province, but throughout India, is remarkable, whilst his resolute and usually successful treatment of dangerous situations renders him valuable to India. Last, but not least, Indians respect him.

I do not think I ever came across a nicer set of men than the Governor's staff, and I shall always retain a grateful recollection of the quiet, well-bred, unobtrusive manner in which they devoted themselves to making me happy and comfortable. I was especially taken with the surgeon, who has the reputation of being one of the best physicians in India. He is a singularly silent man, but his taciturnity was relieved by brilliant flashes of young leopard. He had picked up a leopard cub in the jungle and had brought it up, so far as I could make out, on a diet of sponges and milk. He is devoted to the leopard and the leopard is devoted to him. I took the opportunity on a quiet Sunday morning, when everyone was at church, to pay Mr. Leopard a visit in the large enclosed verandah in which he had his home. He was about the size of a small pointer, and I was fortunate enough to find him in a remarkably amiable frame of mind. I walked with my legs far apart and he kept passing through my legs just as a performing dog does. I do not think he had been trained to do it. I was able to study for the first time a leopard's eyes at close quarters. There is something extraordinarily uncanny about them. They are aquamarine in colour, and whilst you cannot see into them at all you feel as if they look right through you.

On the 19th I passed several hours with Mr. Gokhale and the members of the "Servants of India Society." The "College" buildings are of a superior character; the library is of the very first class, and all the arrangements appear to have been well thought out from every standpoint, including sanitation. The members number fifteen and the permanent assistants five, making twenty-one in all with Mr. Gokhale. All the men I saw, who seemed to be between twenty and thirty years of age, impressed me most favourably. They had frank, open countenances, seemed quite at their ease, spoke with perfect freedom and were altogether as nice a body of young men as I should wish to meet anywhere. I had long conversations with them individually and collectively without Mr. Gokhale being present, and I also had a very long conversation with Mr. Gokhale; but neither from the members of the Society, nor from Mr. Gokhale himself, was I able to receive a clear definition of what the ulterior object of the Society really is. That Mr. Gokhale is trying to create good citizens I have myself no doubt, but the whole plan seems to be visionary, and I suspect that in the end we shall find these men seeking either Government or municipal employment as a means of livelihood. They are highly educated and will no doubt make useful public servants, unless their age, which is somewhat advanced, stands in the way.

On the 22nd I proceeded to Bombay, and it is no exaggeration to say that from 6 o'clock in the morning till past midnight I had not a moment's rest. My movements have been thus chronicled in the *Statesman* of Calcutta:

GOVERNMENT TOURS.

"The Finance Member visited the Bombay Presidency, where the Opium difficulty with China and the Fiscal policy of the Government had met with a good deal of hostile criticism. Sir Guy Fleetwood Wilson visited Poona first and conferred with His Excellency the Governor and others. He also visited among other places the Servants of India Society, of which Mr. Gokhale is the head. At Bombay he was the guest of the Hon. Mr. Monteath, President of the Chamber of Commerce, and had an informal discussion with the Chamber itself on the vexed question of the gold standard reserve and the closing of the mints to rupee coinage. Sir Sassoon David and other Indian merchants met Sir Fleetwood and discussed the question of the Opium trade and urged compensation for losses in Canton owing to the contravention of the Cheefoo Convention and suggested the suspension of Opium sale. The Finance Member was able to assure them that the Government of India had taken a very strong position and would doubtless do their best to enforce the terms of the Cheefoo Convention. The informal Conference which is now discussing the Canton Opium Duty in Peking has before it the views of the Government of India. The Indian merchants also discussed various other questions, including the prospects of the silver market, in which Bombay has for some time now taken a lead. The members of the Exchange also interviewed the Finance Member and discussed several important matters."

One afternoon I accepted an invitation from Mr. Goculdas, who is, I believe, very wealthy and a leading merchant, to attend at his house a garden-party of Bombay Indian merchants who desired to make my acquaintance. I am unable to give the names of the gentlemen who were asked to meet me, but they were representative of the most important Indian financial, commercial, and industrial interests in Bombay, and they numbered about thirty. I was with them the whole afternoon and listened to every conceivable grievance and to every, almost inconceivable, remedy. I was very greatly struck by the high order of intelligence of the Bombay Indian communities. They seem to me to be elbowing out the English. An absorption of English firms by Parsees seems to be going on. I was a good deal heckled, but I received from them all the greatest courtesy and very friendly consideration, and my intercourse with them was both pleasant and advantageous. Indeed, I may say of all those whom I met in Bombay, English or Indian, that nothing could have exceeded their individual and collective kindness, and my visit to Bombay will ever remain one of the brightest and happiest events of my Indian career. I was the guest of charming hosts, Mr. and Mrs. Monteath.

On my way to Bombay I passed Gwalior. I do not think I have ever seen anything finer than the appearance it presents from the railway. It is a large town and fort perched on the top of a high rock, and reminded me somewhat of a gigantic Belvoir castle. I had not travelled through India during the rains before and was much struck by the un-Indian look of the whole country. Instead of parched, dusty districts, the whole country was green and well watered; in fact, the whole of Bombay reminded me more of Hertfordshire in a fine late spring than anything else.

On my return journey I stopped at Jaipur, my object being to visit Amber, the old capital of the State, which is one of the most beautiful and interesting cities in India. I visited the small temple, where a goat is daily offered as the substitute for the human being who, in bygone days, was every morning sacrificed to the god Kali. I did the whole thing in a day, but it was very tiring. There were alternations of torrential rain-storms and roasting sun, and most of the road had to be covered on an elephant. Personally I can stand the jolting of an elephant very well, but there is no doubt that to climb up or down a very steep hill on an elephant is the most fatiguing exercise that anyone can indulge in. I am able, however, to recommend the process as a first-class "cure" for dyspepsia. I only stopped an hour or two in Jaipur; long enough to experience much kindness, both from the Maharajah and from the Political Resident and his charming wife. I visited the School of Art and saw a very large collection of the brass-work for which Jaipur is celebrated, but which does not in the least appeal to me.

My visit to Bombay has left me deeply impressed with the imperative necessity of touring and getting as much as possible into personal touch with the members of the non-official community in the great business centres of India; but with the enormous and ever-increasing volume of work, touring has to be reduced to a minimum.

LETTER XIII.—MADRAS, PONDICHERRY, TRAVANCORE—ELEPHANT AND BISON

CALCUTTA, *December 15th,* 1910.

FOR my cold weather tour I undertook a prolonged and somewhat arduous journey in Southern India, and I hope you will bear with me if I send you a somewhat lengthy account of my doings.

The adaptability of the human frame to violent alternations of temperature presents an interesting study in India. I left Simla on October 25th, and it was so cold there that for a few days before my departure I was sitting by the fire with a shawl over my shoulders. By the time I had got well into the plains I was shedding every garment I could get rid of, and I was, as is usual with me, covered with prickly heat. Calcutta is at that time of year moist, enervating, and disagreeable, but the sun was very hot, which was a great comfort to me.

A short while after leaving Calcutta, I found myself in torrential rain, chilly weather, and a very "sticky" atmosphere. Again, when I got to the extreme South, the heat was intense; and when I reached the high land in Travancore, it was nearly as cold as it had been in Simla. In Europe, if one went straight from England to the South of Italy and from there to Siberia in mid-winter, the chances are one would die of pneumonia.

But somehow or other in India the human frame seems to stand it.

The prospect of a very long journey by train from Calcutta to Madras, and on, filled me with some apprehension, but I am always greatly helped by traversing new country. Anything new carries me along in the most extraordinary way, and I seem to forget boredom and fatigue and all the discomforts incidental to long days and nights in the train. It was the same thing in London. Often have I thoroughly enjoyed a hot, stuffy day in August (when I have been kept in town) simply because I took a long walk in some unknown slum where even the dirty children presented novel features. So it is out here. I suppose it is a matter of temperament, but no one knows how greatly this has helped me in India. Flies, dust, squalor, or discomfort, there is an element of delight in all so long as the flies are fresh flies, the dust is new dust, the squalor is unexplored, and the discomfort novel.

I was intensely pleased with Southern India. The railway traverses most lovely country, green, well-wooded and well-watered—at least, so it was when I went there; and the landscape is diversified by hills of considerable beauty and some height, which is a great relief after the usual flat plains of India. The whole country seemed tidy, well cared for, and pleasanter-looking than the middle and North of India. In Madras the men wear their hair tied in a knot falling on the nape of the neck, and as many of them wear spectacles and flowing garments, they would pass muster for unlovely suffragettes.

One of the features along the railway-line is the Chilka Lake, a vast sheet of brackish water full, I understand, of fish.

I had hoped to travel down to Madras in fair comfort in my saloon, but as usual I came in for a break in the line owing to abnormally heavy and late rains. Equally, as usual, I was assured that both the weather and the break were most exceptional. The whole of Friday afternoon it poured incessantly, a regular monsoon downpour, and we gradually got into country which was practically under water. The only merit in the weather was that it cured my prickly heat.

The ryots in Madras use huge straw umbrellas, which seem to do equally well for sun and rain; at any rate, they all seemed perfectly happy and fairly dry. In the neighbourhood of Waltair the farms and farm steadings might have been English, so well built and so well kept did they seem to be.

At Waltair Junction I got news that the line was washed away some seventy miles north of Madras, and I found myself having to face two deviations and two changes. Seeing that the relief line was built on water-level, it is not surprising that the deviations had been washed away as soon as they were made. I found myself obliged to go a long way round, which involved two changes and a special train. The serious part of it was that I had to unpack in my saloon in a hurry, leave half my things behind, and travel with an irreducible minimum of goods and chattels, clothes and bedding, which in India generally spells a catastrophe. I went through

Trichinopoly, the country round which swarms with parrakeets, or love-birds as they are sometimes called. There were rows upon rows of them sitting upon the telegraph wires just as the swallows do at home, and as the train came up and they flew off, they presented a succession of the most brilliant emerald flashes. The effect was very beautiful. I noticed in this neighbourhood, what I have not seen anywhere else in India, dead crows tied up by the wing and used as scarecrows. The general aspect of the country and the scarecrows gave an English atmosphere to the country to a striking degree.

I reached Madras at 3 o'clock on Saturday and drove straight to Government House, but found no one there but an extremely kind and helpful A.D.C.

I have little to note in connection with my visit to Madras. Immediately after I arrived (on October 29th) I attended a large party given by the Sheriff of Madras to which all the principal official and commercial notabilities of Madras, both Indian and European, were asked to meet me. I was shown marked kindness and consideration by all with whom I came in contact. The garden in which the party was given is singularly beautiful, full of tropical plants, and is the best garden of the kind to be seen in India.

The same day I had interesting interviews with the secretary of the Bank of Madras, and the editor of the *Madras Times*, one of our very best papers. I also interviewed some of my own financial officials.

Madras itself may seem somewhat uninteresting.

There is plenty of elbow-room, no crowd, little noise and a general atmosphere of repose, but it is essentially old India, and therefore attracted me.

I left Madras that evening at about 7 o'clock and travelled through a country which reminded me somewhat of the Karoo Desert in South Africa. I reached Kodaikanal, which is the terminus of the South Indian Railway, about midday on Sunday, and at once started in a bullock cart, or transit as it is called locally, having ordered relays of bullocks all along the fifty-seven miles' drive which I had undertaken to face. Soon after starting, the rain came down in sheets and the road, never a very good one, became atrocious, which of course delayed me. We had to cross two or three small rivers, but we got over them without any disaster. At 10 o'clock at night I reached the Taine River and found it in flood. All my chattels were on the other side of the river, having crossed earlier, and I found myself held up by a broad and raging torrent 10 or 12 feet deep and quite impassable. I had to pass the night in a bare "rest" room. Until next day I had nothing to eat but some chocolate. I never remember a more miserable night in my life. I said the room was bare, but it was fully populated. Amongst other visitors I had a swarm of dragon-flies. If I lighted a small bit of candle which I had with me, they dashed at it and my face. If, on the other hand, I tried darkness, numberless cockroaches took their walks abroad all over me. Numberless fleas and their first cousins were touchingly attentive.

On Monday morning about 12 o'clock the river

had gone down sufficiently to admit of crossing. It was a risky performance. First of all I had to be carried across on the shoulders of coolies. Then followed my beloved rifles. I was much more apprehensive about them than about myself. Then came my small amount of luggage, and finally the bullocks were swum across and the carts were floated across. The local Indian officials of subordinate degree were extraordinarily helpful and the coolies worked grandly, up to their chins in water. I got across without losing anything and without even wetting my feet. I rejoined my people and heavier luggage, and got on to Uttapalayam, where I had some luncheon kindly got ready for me by a young Mr. Vernede, a rubber planter, who had kindly volunteered to pilot me up to the top of the Cardamom Hills, which are really mountains 4,000 feet high, and look after me there. Having got my possessions on the heads of coolies, he and I started for a twenty-mile ride on hill ponies. Within twenty minutes of leaving Uttapalayam a cyclone burst, the worst known for some years in Travancore. It was not rain, it was literally sheets of water that poured down upon us. It also blew a gale of great violence. In two minutes we were soaking wet to the skin. The whole of my effects, including my bedding, rifles, and spare clothes, were soaked. Half-way up the mountains we lost the servants, who had simply collapsed, and by the time we had done a third of the journey, under very great difficulty, it became impossible to ride owing to the torrents having washed away the bridle-paths. There was no help for it, and I had to face twelve miles of cliff climbing *on foot* in torrential rain the whole time. I had to ford three torrents waist-high and in one case I was wet nearly up to my shoulders. Had it been possible, of course I should have turned back, but the valley behind had practically become a sheet of water. I reached my destination, Oodmanshola, more dead than alive. In a bungalow where I was to pass the night, I met Mr. Vernede, senior, who is Magistrate of the district, and who had undertaken to look after me. With him was Mr. Fraser, a tea-planter, and one of the nicest men I have ever come across. Nothing could have exceeded their kindness. They rubbed me dry, wrapped me up in their own warm things, and put me to bed after giving me some soup.

Next day I stopped in bed, feeling very queer, till late in the afternoon, when a slight break in the weather tempted me to stroll a short way on to a conical hill close to the bungalow. I had a telescope with me and I saw the most beautiful sight I have ever seen. It was like being in a huge zoological gardens. I saw two bears playing about like two dogs, romping after each other, rolling over each other, and occasionally giving each other a smack. I saw a small herd of three bison, animals which are becoming rare in India, and what I enjoyed most, seven wild elephants, two of which were babies, or, as they are called here, *batchas*. They were quite unconscious that we were within half a mile of them, and they walked about the long grass tearing at the tree-tops, pulling up bamboos, and generally having a good time of it. The country round reminded me of Guisachan,

Portsmouth's place in Scotland, on a huge scale. I was only able to be out a very short time, as again the rain came down in torrents. During the whole of the ten days during which I was on the top of the mountain, it never ceased raining hard except on two mornings, and then for about four hours only each time. One day was Wednesday the 2nd, when I started off with Fraser and young Vernede in the hope of getting a bison. I was stiff with rheumatism, and of course crippled owing to my knee, and even on the hill-top it was very difficult for me to get about.

After spying some little time we located a bull bison down in the valley. He was at the edge of the jungle, and it was quite hopeless for me to attempt to go after him. Possibly a young and very active man might, by running two miles, have got round him before he worked back to the jungle, but I doubt it, as the wind was against it. So in despair I had to give him up. Presently, however, I made out another bison nearer and lying down in the long grass. It was impossible to shoot him where he was, and the wind did not admit of my getting up to him, so we decided to wait in hopes that he might graze up the hill towards us, which bison not infrequently do. We came away, as we thought it best to leave him severely alone till he felt inclined to move of his own accord, and as we crept away to the other side of the hill-top, I caught sight of two points, evidently of horns. I had my rifle in my hand, and I made a rush forward and found myself within 30 yards of a bull bison, three cows and a calf. There was not a second to lose. They gave me one look and I think the bull meant to "go for" me. Bison are dangerous when wounded or when they have calves about them. I was above him, and aiming between his horns, I tried to hit him in the middle of the withers and succeeded. He fell as if struck by lightning and died as I got up to him. I never was more gratified in my life. Everyone in India had told me that it was very difficult for anyone to get a bison, and impossible for a crippled old man to do so. I have got my bison and a good one. He was a seven-year-old bull, so at least they told me, with a very nice head. A bull bison is quite the most beautiful animal I have ever seen. This one stood about 18 hands at the shoulder. The coat is black-brown, and all four legs are white or cream colour. He looked like a gigantic prize bull at Smithfield. I am indeed glad to have obtained such a fine trophy. I then went back to the other side of the hill to see what had happened to the bull that was lying down.

My shot had disturbed him and he was trotting away through the very long grass. I tried him, although the shooting was extremely difficult. My first shot went just over him, but my second, well over 300 yards, hit him and wounded him severely. I should undoubtedly have got him that afternoon but for the fact that he was at the edge of a jungle into which he worked, and where the "grass" was some 12 feet high (grass is really cane), and where it would have been perfectly useless to go after him as well as very dangerous. I, of course, could not get down there on account of my leg, and the shikaris refused to go up to him,

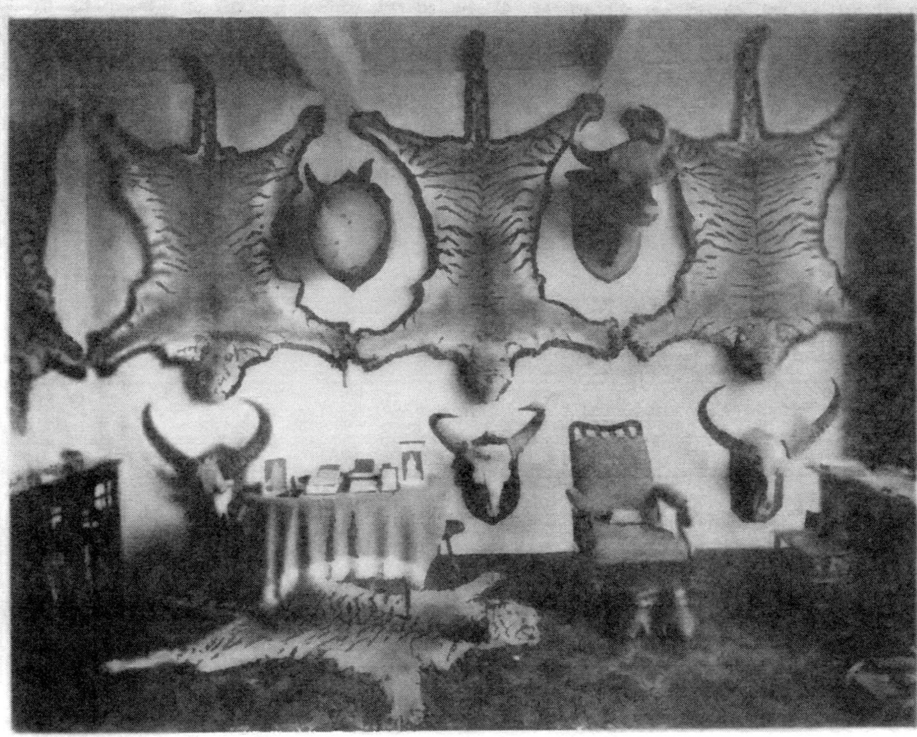

Photo: Mr. King.

OLD FRIENDS.

as it would have been quite useless, inasmuch as the grass would have been many feet above their heads and it would have been impossible to shoot. I am very sorry I lost him, both because he was a fine bull, and because I cannot bear to let a wounded beast linger in pain. He was, I suppose, eaten in the night by hunting dogs or jackals.

Next day we had to move on to another camp. It was a very punishing operation for me. We had to ford three torrents, one very deep one across which we had to swim the horses. My servants, who joined us at the first bungalow, were absolutely numbed with wet and cold and quite useless for the rest of the time they were with me, and I myself was done up. Every bungalow, whether pukka-built—that is, of baked brick—or built of bamboo, has to be surrounded by an elephant trench about 8 feet deep and 8 feet broad, as the elephants destroy bungalows if they can get at them. It is on account of the elephants that there are no bridges. As soon as a bridge is put up an elephant looks at it with some curiosity, and then proceeds to demolish it.

I reached my second camp after a twelve-mile ride, again soaked to the skin, and I found the tiny house in which I had to live was made entirely of bamboos, very similar to the Japanese bamboo houses, beautifully built and quite weather-tight, but covered with mildew and extremely damp in such weather as we were enjoying. Here we were locked in by torrential rain till Tuesday, November 8th, when in the morning there was again a break in the weather, the break lasting for about four hours as on the previous occasion.

The evening before, just at sunset, two men, a post-runner and the Magistrate's clerk, had come in looking scared out of their wits, and told us that a rogue elephant had chased them for two miles and kept them up in a tree for some time. I immediately asked Mr. Vernede to send two of the hillmen to follow the elephant, to stop with him all night, and then one of the two was to come and tell us in the morning at daybreak where the elephant was. Mercifully the weather improved, and at daybreak next morning a man came in to say that the elephant was grazing alone on the edge of a marsh about two miles off. We got off immediately, and after about three miles up and down hills we got on to a sugar-loaf top, and from there we saw a sight I shall never forget. I do not think I could have seen less than fifty elephants. There were three herds in different directions, males, females and calves, but they had got our wind, and soon the herds were all going in a stately procession in different directions and away from us. We made out, however, our solitary bull. He was still feeding at the edge of the marsh. Then we sat down and had a long and anxious consultation as to the best way to get at him. Eventually we decided to make a large circuit and get to the opposite side of the marsh, where there was a very large boulder of rock, almost a small hill. We also decided that the only possible way I could get him, if I were prepared to face the music, was to come suddenly round the boulder and walk straight into the marsh as near as the elephant would let me get to him, and try and shoot him through the brain. I had said nothing about it to my friends because I was afraid they would insist on keeping me in bed, but every night I had had an attack of fever, and that, coupled with my rheumatism, made it impossible for me to lift my elephant rifle, a magnificent ·8 bore weighing some 16 pounds. I accordingly decided to trust to my ·465 Holland—a beautiful weapon, but hardly as suitable for so big a beast as an elephant as my ·8 bore. I must say that both Vernede and Fraser behaved beautifully to me. Some men would have flatly refused to let me undertake what I made up my mind to do. We had a considerable tramp before we got down to the boulder, and then I did what I had decided to do. I came quickly round the side of the hill and went straight into the marsh towards the elephant; Fraser and Vernede did likewise away to my left. I was well above my knees in mud, water and rushes, and most awkwardly placed for shooting, inasmuch as the elephant was on ground considerably higher than the level of the marsh. It is always very dangerous to shoot at a wild beast when he is above you—in fact, it is a recognised rule never to do so; but this was the only chance of my life of getting an elephant, and I determined to risk everything to get him. When I had got to within 40 yards of him he appeared inclined to charge me. Up to then he had looked at me very much as though I were an interesting beetle. The situation seemed to me so extraordinarily comical that I nearly burst out laughing. Across the narrow marsh stood the elephant on rising ground, looking at me about as viciously as any beast could. He was known to be a rogue and reputed to have killed three men during the last two years. He had repeatedly chased natives and had done a good deal of destruction in the way of damaging their crops and their huts. About the middle of the marsh and only some 40 yards from him, immovable owing to the mud, stood an old gentleman full of fever and rheumatism, with large gold spectacles on his nose and a too light rifle in his hands. As I have said, I felt an irresistible desire to laugh, the whole thing seemed so comical.

I took the steadiest aim I could, and my direction was perfectly correct, but I shot a bit too high. I knew I was doing so, but I could not help it owing to the elephant standing so much above me. To have fired lower would have been to hit him in the trunk, and I dared not take any risks. Vernede told me afterward that I had hit him in what is known as the brain-box, the spongy, bony case which holds the brain, but I think I must have scraped his brain as well, because he stood as though suddenly paralysed. I gave him a second shot very near the first with my second barrel, again unavoidably firing a bit too high, but it was sufficient for him. The elephant turned round and with difficulty climbed the bank behind him. I frankly confess to feeling a sense of relief when I saw that he had given up the idea of charging, for with the light rifle I had, nothing could have stopped him. As he lifted his fore-leg on to the higher ground I let him have a bullet behind the shoulder. Up to then no one had fired but myself, but I called out to Vernede to give him a shot from my heavy ·8 bore rifle, as I was so afraid of losing him. Vernede and Fraser each placed a bullet in exactly the right spot just as the elephant crashed into the jungle.

Before we started and on more than one other occasion we had discussed the grave impropriety of going after any wounded animal in long grass. By long grass I mean a species of cane which grows to some 20 feet in height. We condemned as dangerous maniacs with a suicidal tendency men who did such a thing, and we assured one another that under no conditions should we be guilty of such folly. So far so good, but the moment the elephant dived into the long grass, we were all three after him exactly like a pack of hounds dashing into a gorse covert. To my intense gratification we found the elephant lying on his side stone dead some 50 yards from where I had shot him. I myself think that he might have gone a bit farther but for Vernede's shot from my ·8 bore, but they both declared that had I not mortally wounded him, he would most certainly have killed me or been quite a mile away from the spot a few minutes after I had fired. Be that as it may, I got my elephant, and he proved to be the possessor of two very nice tusks. I never shall forget the sensation I experienced when I stood by the huge dead beast. He measured 8 feet 4 inches at the shoulder; he was in splendid condition and was a heavily built animal. My first feeling was of extreme regret at having killed him, but afterwards I felt fully justified and much comforted by the knowledge that he was a proclaimed brute who had committed murder, and who certainly would have gone on killing had he not been put out of the way. Still, I do not think I should care to shoot another, glad as I am to have got one. I must say I was rather gratified to have shot both my bison and my elephant on foot and in perfectly open ground. I suppose if I stop here much longer I am bound to be pinched, as shooting on foot is undoubtedly dangerous. But in my opinion there is no sport like it in the world, and it has completely spoilt me for shooting from a *machân* or from a howdah. It is the danger and the dependence on one's own steadiness and straight shooting which is so attractive.

I had gone up to the Cardamom Hills from one end of the range, and having crossed from one end to the other, a matter of some hundred miles, I descended into the plain at the other end and came down a precipitous path into Cumbur Valley, a magnificent, well-watered and highly cultivated plain of great extent, lying between the two ranges. In Cumbur I lunched at the house of a native timber merchant, who has most considerately built a bungalow for the use of Europeans who may be travelling in that part of the country. From Cumbur I rode to the next rest-house, where I passed the night, recrossing the Taine River, and made my way back to Kodaikanal, which I reached on Saturday the 12th after a most exhausting bullock transit journey of some sixty miles. My next stopping-place was Madura, celebrated for its temple, one of the most sacred, and certainly the most imposing I have seen in India. There are two temples much in the same style, one being used as a market. The stone carvings are on a gigantic scale and very striking, but both the temples and the town are extremely dirty. The day was very hot and the smells were very nasty, but Madura is well worth a visit, the temples being certainly the finest in the South, if not in the whole of India. The sacred tank is also worth seeing, but it entails a drive into the country, which, however, I faced tired though I was.

From Madura I went on to the French colony of Pondicherry. Beyond having a typical French officer at the head of the police—one of the smartest-looking men, be it said, that I have seen in India, and the possessor of a very smart, pretty little wife—there is nothing especially French about Pondicherry, except a swarm of French priests. The pier is nearly as good as Brighton Pier, and the approach to it is beautified by a number of very fine columns which the French have looted from some temple in the interior. There is also a fine sea walk with a parapet, well worthy of a first-class watering-place, but there is nothing else except a row of large warehouses, which when I was there were filled with ground-nuts, which represent the only trade, I am told, export or import, which Pondicherry enjoys, the said ground-nuts all going to Marseilles, where *on dit* they produce what the public is made to swallow as the " best olive oil."

From Pondicherry I made my way back to Madras, which I reached on Monday morning. In Madras I had two interesting interviews with the Chamber of Commerce and with the Associated Trades of Madras. I make a point of interviewing every member of any importance of the financial, commercial, and industrial communities of India wherever I go. I think they like it, and I am sure I derive considerable advantage from it. Madras was no exception. I was most kindly treated by the two bodies I have mentioned, and I shall always look back to my visit to Madras as a most pleasant and highly instructive experience.

I then repeated my long, tedious, and, owing to the floods, frequently broken journey to Calcutta, which I reached on November 16th, and which I found busy preparing for the departure of the Mintos and the arrival of the Hardinges. By the time I reached my house I was, to use a vulgar expression, "fairly cooked," and I am only now beginning to recover from the fatigue, the exposure, and the atrocious weather which I have experienced. But all are overshadowed by my two trophies and the great charm of Southern India.

Ever shall I remember the kindness, the help, and the consideration which I received in Travancore from the two Vernedes and Fraser, and the pair of beautiful tusks will always remind me of the generous hospitality of His Highness the Maharajah of Travancore.

LETTER XIV.—BAY OF BENGAL AND TIGER-DRIVING

CALCUTTA, *December 31st*, 1910.

I KNOW of nothing more annoying than to be unable to attribute to others blame which properly attaches to oneself. I have for some weeks been suffering acutely from neuritis. I should much like to attribute it to the topographical configuration of my official or private abode, to the carelessness of my servants, or, better still, to the very detestable electric fans which shorten life in India, and which my friends and enemies persist in letting loose in the neighbourhood of my hairless head. I am compelled in lieu thereof to admit that the pain I have been suffering is solely and entirely attributable to the exposure and fatigue which I underwent in Travancore. *Il faut souffrir pour être* the possessor of tusks and horns. Neuritis plus the loss of that prince of tiger-shoot *bandobasters*, Meyer (who has had to devote this cold weather to organising sport for Ashby St. Leger), induced me, for once, to consider my health. Accordingly I decided to indulge in a mild yachting trip and shut my eyes when I glanced in the direction of my rifles. Sir Edward Baker had most kindly placed a Forest Department launch, the *Hawk*, at my disposal, and in it I have been cruising about the Bay of Bengal. It has not relieved me of pain, but I think my general health has greatly improved, so I have gained that much to the good.

I left Calcutta on Friday, December 16th, after attending the last Council of this year, and boarded the *Hawk* at Khulna. We steamed all day through several of the beautiful Sunderbund *khals*. till we reached Tiger Point, which is on the estuary known as Horngotta Road, which opens on to the Bay of Bengal. Just above Tiger Point is Rhino Point. The names are to be found in an old map in my possession dated 1809, but I think the places have been rechristened in the latter-day ones. The old names are indicative of the then game-producing nature of the localities. Rhinoceroses are quite extinct in the Sunderbunds, and although tigers abound, they frequent the dense jungles inland, following the cheetal deer, however, when the latter come down to the short grass and salt-licks along the shore. Just now there is a shortage of deer owing to so many having been drowned during the "bore" of last year. Three drowned tigers were then seen floating down the rivers. Khulna tigers have a bad reputation. They have quite lost all fear of man, and if cheetal are short, become man-eaters. I understand that the death-roll in the Sunderbunds exceeds one hundred per annum. These are the actually reported deaths, but no doubt many unrecorded ones occur besides. The Forest Department coolies are the chief sufferers, and there is no doubt that in the Khulna District tigers have established a veritable reign of terror. The nature of the ground, dense bamboo jungle with slimy mud foundation and intersected by small *khals*, makes it extremely difficult to effect their destruction. They seem to be much more cunning than Central and United Provinces tigers, and are rarely caught in traps. I heard of one tigress who was bogged in the mud and killed with spears, but she was old and weak. I believe it is an established fact that on one occasion a tiger was run into and killed by a steamer whilst he was swimming across a river; and I have been told of one tiger who was caught in fishing-nets. The tiger had strayed on to a long tongue of dry sand jutting out into the bay. A crowd of fishing-boats mobbed him and he blundered into a set of nets spread out for him at the shore end of the spur. He soon tied himself up in a mass of netting and lay exhausted and helpless. Just at this moment a missionary parson turned up by the merest accident and begged to be allowed to shoot the tiger. The fishermen had an old musket and agreed to let the padre finish off the tiger. So absolutely ignorant of fire-arms was he that someone had to hold the musket whilst he pulled the trigger. I have no doubt that *more Anglico Indico* he is now alluded to as the greatest shikari in Bengal, who "always shoots his tigers on foot and at close quarters." I dare say the whole story is a canard.

A *réputation volée* is very easily acquired in India. A youth cribs from a German article on, say, the "bellicosity of blue butterflies," and writes a report thereon. He is at once dubbed the greatest authority on the subject in Delhi, later on in the Punjab; lastly he is pronounced to be the greatest authority on lepidoptera in India, "if not in the world," and no one dreams of questioning his claims to fame. Possibly he is promoted on the strength of them.

In the Sunderbunds tigers are, as a rule, shot over a "kill" or over a fresh-water hole near a tree. I never attempted this, first because from a sporting standpoint the system does not appeal to me, and secondly because I dared not run the risk of the subsequent, almost inevitable attack of malarial fever; but I have tried to walk them up in long grass—a dangerous proceeding and one not to be recommended to the jumpy or to any but very reliable shots.

When on tour I always take my rifles with me, and I had also with me some marriage-festival bombs. These are easy to make. A little gun-powder is wrapped up in paper and jute fibre is wound tightly round the packet till a sphere about the size of a cricket-ball is produced. Into it a short piece of very thin reed is inserted into which a pinch of fine powder is poured, thus furnishing a touch-match. The reed is lighted with a lucifer match and the bomb is thrown as far as possible. It bursts on the ground, making a very loud detonation. Of course, such bombs can only be used in damp localities, where there is no danger of setting the jungle on fire.

We reached Tiger Point late on Saturday evening and landed next morning. The coast reminded me vividly of the Portland, Swanage, and Bournemouth coast-line in Dorsetshire. The vegetation, however, was very distinctly Eastern. The beach was of fine white, dazzling sand backed by sand-dunes, behind which came a long strip of high grass, or of reeds known as tiger-grass, and behind that was a maidan of short grass backed by dense jungle, bounded by a sluggish smelly *khal*—an ideal place for cheetal and tiger. The sandy shore was covered with numberless small sealing-wax-red crabs such as I had never seen before. Their name I have been unable to ascertain. As the crabs ran with amazing rapidity, I at once, with that brilliancy which characterises my every utterance, christened them "scarlet-runners." The effect of numberless shining scarlet spots on the white sand was beautiful. It was hard to realise that the innocent-looking, placid bay is full of sharks, muggers (crocodiles), and venomous snakes. The bay teems with edible fish; one small, dace-like kind incessantly takes continuous leaps out of the water and frequently jumps into boats.

Carefully inspecting the ground, I soon came upon tiger pugs and from what I saw I judged that a tiger, tigress, and *batcha* either lived on or frequented this tongue of land. The ground was next to impossible to beat, but I determined to try. If I allude to what had been done by way of "helping" me, I do so not in any spirit of angry criticism, but because it may be useful to others to know what not to do. I have rarely seen so much of that "what" in so concentrated a form as on this occasion. The Deputy-Conservator of Forests had, with the best intentions, sent one of his subordinates to "keep the place quiet," and that unfortunate person had done so with a vengeance. *L'homme propose*, and in this case the youth void of understanding disposed. "Now let me show you what I have done," the young man remarked with some pride, and to my horror and utter dismay he showed us paths cut through every covert, trees felled "where they were likely to be in the way," grass beaten down "to make it easier to get along," and to cap all he had erected seven of the most grotesque *machâns* I have ever had the misfortune to set eyes on.

What he had succeeded in doing was to clear the ground of every mortal thing which might have been on it. For an accursed week he had had some thirty coolies at work chopping, digging, shouting, lighting fires and I know not what else.

Mercifully I was too crushed to speak. Had I been able to do so, my language would doubtless have brought on a thunder-storm.

The *machâns* which had been erected were a sight for the gods. There were seven of them, all erected in the very places which should have been left severely alone for a tiger to creep along. All were actually above the sky-line, regular scare-crow sky-scrapers, calculated to clear the country of game of all kinds and quite impossible to shoot from. I think they must have been 50 or 60 feet in the air. To complete the disastrous arrangement, huge ladders of staring yellow bamboos were fixed against the trees, quite enough in themselves to turn any beast. The poor youth had had the sticks of the trays laid all one way instead of butt to base, and had used thin, dry, brittle sticks. The whole machine was as dangerous as it was useless.

He induced me to climb up into one, and pointed

with the air and attitude of a Napoleon to broad naked patches of ground which no earthly tiger would dream of crossing, and proudly remarked that his *machân* commanded "all the open ground." It commanded all the open sea as well, for that matter.

Opinions vary as to the safe height for *machâns*. I myself utterly disbelieve all the stories told about tigers springing up at or on to *machâns* or climbing trees.

The first and natural effort of a wounded tiger is to *get away*. It is when he is shot at again, or followed or cut off, that he charges. But in any case a badly wounded tiger would be quite unequal to climbing a tree or "springing up into" a *machân*.

For ordinary mortals 10 or 12 feet is, I think, a perfectly safe height. Additional feet to be added at a progressional rate for all that is especially precious—*e.g.*, women, etc.—till the regulation 25 feet for a sacrosanct Viceroy is reached. Personally I like to be about 10 feet up, but I have been quite happy at 5. Tigers seldom look up and rarely see anything 5 feet above them.

Obviously a *machân* should be so constructed and placed as to look as much as possible like an integral part of the tree. In a treeless bamboo country the only plan possible is to erect a tripod of three solid bamboos.

On the whole, unless the wait is likely to be a very long one, I prefer a light ladder of inconspicuous material tied against a tree-trunk. One can quite well sit on and shoot from one of the top rungs. It can be made *in situ*, is easily carried, and takes no time to fix. It is, of course, unsuitable for sitting over "kills" or water.

I knew nothing would return under at least a week, so I sat me down in patience, though my soul was consumed with vexation.

The weather was ideal and the shore perfection so far as strolling about went, and bitterly disappointed though I was, I enjoyed going about the place, generally quite alone, from dawn to dusk.

I also enjoyed being silently paddled up the numerous narrow *khals*, which always afford a certain amount of interest, although in this part of the Sunderbunds animal life is practically limited to tiger and cheetal, and bird life to herons and kingfishers.

I saw many specimens of the Guisab lizard, one quite 6 feet long and more like a small crocodile than a lizard. The Indians pronounce them to be venomous, but in point of fact they are perfectly harmless. The sailors killed a large black snake some 7 feet long.

On Monday I landed and had a hot and exhausting day walking in long grass on sand and in jungle, selecting places at which to tie up. I had to see to everything myself, and I found it very trying to hobble about all day in a broiling sun with a rifle in one hand and a stick in the other. On Tuesday the Collector of the District turned up in his launch, most kindly coming to see if he could be of any use to me.

I liked Mr. Bradley Birt. He seems to me to be a clever, cultured man with ideas, liberal-minded and in sympathy with the natives. He shares my "Sunderbunds infatuation," and is devoid of that cast-iron uniformity which spoils so many good men in India. He left us the same evening.

The next arrival was a boy of the name of Lewis, just arrived from England on appointment to the Forest Service. A remarkably nice young man.

On Tuesday and Wednesday I had some calves tied up about the jungle at the spots I had selected, in the hope that their smell and their lowing might induce some strolling tiger to kill. It is curious how many Englishmen pass half their lives in India without ever getting "up to" the tricks of our dusky fellow-subjects.

When there has been no kill the cows are brought in at dawn to be watered and tethered out to graze. The day after my arrival one had "got lost." As the ground was water-bound, I assumed the cow would soon be found, and made no "row." Next day a second cow had "got lost." I then felt certain that the good old game of "cow-pinching" was being tried on me. It is a favourite one during shooting expeditions. Unless the ryots are made to find the first "lost" animal, which has generally been tucked away to be "found" after the Sahib's departure, they will gradually "lose" half a dozen. This is a very common piece of rascality. I sent a *chaprassie* to tell the coolies, thirty-two of them, to land at once and search for the cows. He failed to induce them to go. I was so furious at this baby mutiny that I got into the dingy just as I stood. I had nothing on but pyjamas and slippers. When I reached the two big native house-boats I ordered the coolies to land, but the headman declined to move, saying he was cooking his dinner. I dived into the middle of them, and the effect was very much that which follows the entry of a ferret into a rabbit-burrow. I had the lot on shore in five minutes. In India, as in other places, resistance to a distinct order must be checked at once, and firmly, or it will spread like wildfire and soon become uncontrollable. Not another cow was "lost" during the trip.

On Friday morning (December 23rd) we got *khubber* of a kill. I was overjoyed and much surprised. We landed at 9 o'clock, my stock-in-trade consisting of a box of bombs and twenty-four boxes of lucifer matches; also a short bamboo ladder from off the launch.

At the risk of wearying you I shall now describe my *modus operandi*. Having carefully considered the line taken by the tiger as evidenced by the "drag"—and it is curious what little trace a tiger leaves when dragging even a heavy cow or buffalo—and studied the likely places, we came to the conclusion that he had taken the kill into a dense shrubbery of kola bush on the *khal* side of the maidan. The tiger-grass was intact, as was the other long grass, and I could find no tracks round other kola bushes. So we located him as I have described, and as it turned out we located him correctly. Next, very silently and with great circumspection, for we might be charged by or blunder on to the tiger at any moment, we crept through the jungle which headed the maidan and selected three trees for our occupation.

I put young Lewis in a large tree on the sea-front side, whilst the Deputy-Conservator climbed to the top of a smaller tree, too high in my opinion either to see or to shoot satisfactorily; but that was his concern. The tree was well on our proper left. I myself selected a tree (in the centre) growing by a cheetal path which I thought the tiger might take to. I then went back to the thirty-four beaters and had them lined from the shore end of the maidan to as far as I could induce them to go towards the dense jungle flanking the *khal*. To each man I gave eight bombs and a box of matches.

As soon as I got back to my tree—and I must confess that this crossing and recrossing the long grass in the vicinity of the tiger was trying—I put the bamboo ladder against it and sent the one man I had taken with me back to the line to start the beaters. I found that the tree did not admit of my sitting higher than on the fourth rung of the ladder, the spreading branches obstructing my view if I sat higher. Four feet from the ground is a *leetle* low when a tiger is being beaten *towards* one, but I had to come low, as the bamboo ladder creaked so loudly that it would have turned any animal coming in its direction. I stood on the ground beside it counting on having time to climb the ladder if I wounded the tiger. I could not well miss him in the path. The sun was very hot and we were at work in the hottest part of the day. I was tired out and to this I attribute my one mistake. I made but one, I think, but it cost us the tiger, although I am not quite satisfied that the tiger could not have been shot in spite of it. I forgot to put a couple of men in trees on the *khal* side of the jungle to tap and so keep the tiger well in the middle of us. I cannot imagine how I came to forget it, but I had the whole *bandobast* on my shoulders. I had immense difficulties to contend with and I could not speak a word of Bengali; I had no one with me who had the remotest notion of what to do and what to avoid, and the ground was an almost impossible place to beat without three times as many beaters as we had got. Last but not least, I was, towards the end, very, very tired. To give some idea of the amount of labour and preparation involved as well as of the distance from our base, I may say that we left the launch at 9 a.m. and that the first bomb exploded at 1.45. The beaters on the whole, and considering that they were nervous and absolutely inexperienced, kept good line and fired bombs steadily and as instructed.

The tiger broke and passed silently some 20 yards to the left of the third gun, who failed to see it, as he was "looking to his right." Be that as it may, the tiger slipped past him. That is where my mistake cost us so dear. Tappers would almost certainly have pushed the tiger between us instead of letting him slip past just outside us.

I had never before attempted to plan and execute a drive unaided, and I must admit that I was highly gratified to have got a tiger right up to my guns on such ground and in such circumstances.

I am prouder of that day's work than of anything I have done in India.

It will doubtless be remarked that I have done nothing else to be proud of.

On Saturday we steamed to a place called

Dubba, the trip occupying about six hours. We anchored at the mouth of a *khal* facing the Bay of Bengal, a lovely spot, and landed early. We walked about the sand-hills and over an extensive maidan, seeing a few cheetal and coming on one or two stale tiger pugs.

Not many men can tell the " age " of tiger pugs. I have often been assured that the pugs were " quite fresh," when they were obviously several days old. Heavy dew will make a stale pug look fresh and half-an-hour of sun will " bake " a fresh one and make it look a week old. Wind will " blur " a fresh pug in sand in a few minutes. Constant study alone enables a man to "read" a pug with any approach to accuracy. I revel in studying pugs, tracking having always fascinated me. I have dabbled in it ever since I was twelve years old. I know it is heretical to say so, but I do not consider the Indians to be first-class trackers, not excepting even the jungli folk. I give my opinion for what it is worth, but I do not think the Indian tracker is comparable to a really first-class Italian tracker of the Maremma.

It was in the Pyrenees that I first became acquainted with a neat shikar swindle, one which is frequently indulged in by the Indian ryots. In the Pyrenees it is a case of bear footprints, in India of tiger pugs. In both countries the swindle is eminently successful when practised on unsuspecting and inexperienced Englishmen. The method adopted is as follows: When a good clear impression of a tiger's foot is found in stiff soil or clay, a large clod is cut out and placed in the sun till it is baked. An impression is then taken with a piece of soft, well-kneaded clay, and that in turn is baked in the sun. You then have what is practically a tiger's foot in terra-cotta. Many a flat has been induced to pay for *khubber* of tiger by the simple expedient of pressing the shape into soft earth or sand at intervals. I once bought such a clay foot in a bazaar in Calcutta!

On one occasion a wily native tried the trick on me, but I almost immediately detected the uniformity of pressure, which cannot, of course, occur in the case of a live tread.

On Christmas Day young Lewis and I quartered the best part of the maidan, and I was greatly pleased with the cool courage he displayed in following me in and through long grass and by shrubberies of kola such as tigers love to lie up in. He had only landed from England the week before, the place was a *terra incognita* to us both, and tigers had evidently been about the place; but he took his risk "like a man," moving about quietly, coolly, and observantly. The last is an essential quality in a shikari.

Monday, December 26th, I passed strolling lazily along the *khal* bank—a veritable Bank Holiday.

On Tuesday my two companions went off "forestering" in the steam-cutter. To practise forestry from a steam-cutter may sound strange, but Anglo-Indians have weird customs. For instance, the headquarters of the Inspector of Submarine Mining, also of the Inspector of Coast Defences, are at Simla, some 8,000 feet up a mountain four days from the coast; and all for the good of the service, *bien entendu*.

I devoted the day to exploring two new small maidans in the hope of walking up a tiger. I saw nothing but some cheetal does.

Thus ended my Christmas holiday in the year of grace 1910.

Had Tiger Point been left undisturbed, had I had anyone with me acquainted with the first principles of shikar, and had I been supplied with sufficient beaters, I believe I should have met with some measure of success.

I returned to Calcutta a healthier if a sadder man, and my eyes were gladdened on arrival by the sight of the head of my Travancore second bull bison, which had been found dead not far from where I shot it. He was a superb specimen.

I at once addressed it in the words of Mr. Punch:

> " Your headpiece cured and mounted shall record,
> And be the cynosure of envious men."

LETTER XV.—PARLIAMENTARY YEAR, 1911

CALCUTTA, *April*, 1911.

THE Parliamentary year which has just closed has unmasked the batteries, and it may interest you to know what impression I have received as regards trouble in the future.

Generally speaking, the Indian members have given evidence of a marked aptitude for debate, a quite remarkable respect for order, and a courteous attitude beyond praise.

The two most prominent members are Mr. Gokhale, who is a real power in the Chamber, as he always has been out of it. The other is the absolutely irreconcilable pundit Malaviya. The latter is always a bitter critic unable to recognise any good in anything done or proposed by the Government. Injudicious handling of him will turn him into a source of some danger.

Mr. Gokhale, on the other hand, has given expression to broad statesmanlike views and is scrupulously fair in debates. His support when it can be obtained is invaluable, for he is a veritable triton among the minnows.

The Indians as a whole, and almost of necessity, constitute the "Opposition," but their attitude is constructive as well as iconoclastic.

The quality of the speeches, as a whole, is quite up to the standard of most representative Chambers, whilst some are quite above average.

Those on important resolutions on public expenditure and the tariff, the cost of the Army, Hindoo marriage law, sanitation, railways, and notably on Excise cotton duties, sedition, and education, have been excellent, and indicate careful and even profound study of the subjects dealt with.

The danger ahead appears to lie in a demand for exaggerated expenditure on education, and especially for a reduction in the cost of the Army, as to which all Indians are very sensitive.

They contend that a larger Army is maintained than the needs of India justify, and whilst willing to supply troops for expeditions undertaken for the welfare of India, they bitterly resent having to maintain in peace-time an Army the strength of which is fixed by the policy that Indian troops should always be available for wars undertaken for the benefit of England.

In the event of a big Imperial War I am absolutely certain that India would cheerfully bear almost any burden, but wars such as the South African War will strain their loyalty. This was made abundantly evident during the debate on the strength and cost of the Army.

Mr. Gokhale "rubbed in" that General Brackenbury, who had been Military Member of Council, stated in 1897 in his evidence before the Royal Commission on Indian Expenditure that the strength of the Indian Army was in excess of Indian requirements, and that the Army Commission of 1879, of which Lord Roberts was a member, held that the strength of the Indian Army—60,000 British and 120,000 Indian troops—was sufficient to resist Russian aggression, not only if Russia acted alone but even with Afghanistan as an ally. He then commented on the despatch of troops from India during the South African and China Wars.

The pundit Malaviya unearthed two dissents by Sir Auckland Colvin and Sir Courtenay Ilbert, when members of the Government of India, against the addition in 1886 of 10,000 British and 20,000 Indian troops to the Army.

I have not been able to verify these references, but I am assured that they are correct.

Ancient history no doubt, but sufficiently to the point to show that the despatch of troops from India on " adventures " will be a dangerous policy to the future.

A pleasant note was sounded by Mr. Mazhural Hague, who said:

" Sir Guy Fleetwood Wilson in introducing his Budget expressed a hope that the provision of £940,000 for the Durbar expenses of His Majesty the King-Emperor will not be considered by the Council as higher than the people of India would wish to provide for the becoming celebration of a great historic event. I assure my Honourable Friend, and through him the whole British nation, that we do not consider the sum at all too high. Indeed, we would have cheerfully borne the expenditure of a much larger amount, even the whole surplus of the present year if necessary, for a grand and befitting reception of our beloved King-Emperor."

In 1909, when I introduced my first Budget in the unreformed Council, I said that I did not fear the impending changes, and that I believed that the inevitably increased and more searching criticism would not be the outcome of any desire to embarrass a Finance Minister honestly striving to do his duty. I am bound to say that my anticipations have proved correct. I have found the criticisms of the non-official members temperate, suggestive, and friendly in tone. The free interchange of views which the reformed and consequently enlarged Council stimulates, is becoming a powerful factor for good in the financial policy of India.

So far all goes well; but it is idle to suppose and childish to expect that educated Indians will long tolerate a system which grants their political representatives the right and the power to discuss almost any proposal, to formulate reasonable demands, to agree in regard to them, and then to have them crushed out of existence by the mechanical vote of a large official majority.

Since Lord Hardinge assumed the reins of office the weekly meetings (an unwritten but well-recognised rule ignored by Lord Minto) have been resumed with immense advantage to the Government and the country. There is now continuity and correlation in administration and a fuller sense of responsibility in the members of the Supreme Council. They now are better able to control their Departments and government by bureaucracy has been reduced. Hardinge governs with and through his Council instead of outside it, with the result that he can absolutely count on support in time of need.

Having been Private Secretary to five or six

Cabinet Ministers, and having, I honestly believe, enjoyed their complete confidence, I have been for many years in close touch with the Cabinets at Home, and so far as I am able to judge, our Indian Council works very much as does the English Cabinet. We, also, have our differences and dissents, but a capable and sensible Governor-General can always count on the support of a large majority of his Council over which he merely presides, his vote counting for no more than do those of the other members. In Council the Governor-General becomes a "colleague."

When the decision of Council has to be recorded, the President calls on the last joined member to speak first, the next junior to speak next, and so on, the senior member expressing his opinion last. The intention is that the younger members should not be "over-awed" by their seniors. The plan works excellently and is, I am told, based on the practice which prevailed at the meetings of the old East India Company's Board. The Commander-in-Chief is an "extraordinary" member and, theoretically, only participates in the discussion of military matters. In practice his opinion is given, and is both sought and welcomed, on any matter in which he takes an interest.

From an "Englishman's" standpoint the great flaw in the Indian Governmental system lies in the fact that the "Secretaries to Government," the equivalent of our Under-Secretaries of State, take the "file" (papers) which are to come under discussion direct to the Viceroy before the Council sits and discuss the question at issue with him in private. There is a twofold objection to this method. It may in certain conditions enable a Secretary to intrigue against his Chief, and it offers him the great temptation to indulge in wholesale agreement with the Viceroy, on whom his advancement depends.

Nothing but the conspicuous loyalty of the Indian Civil Servant has obviated a break-up of a machinery which combines in a Viceroy the dual functions of a Sovereign and a Prime Minister, and enables a permanent official to influence him, should he wish to do so, against the Minister in charge of the Department concerned.

Personally, I readily confess I never experienced a shadow of a difficulty. My Secretaries to Government and myself were as one.

I well remember the first time I became possessed of a Cabinet secret at Home.

There was some trouble just then in the Cabinet. The Government was admittedly somewhat "dicky," and the interchange of Cabinet boxes was fast and furious.

There was also racing at Newmarket, and Hartington rarely allowed anything to interfere with Newmarket and to Newmarket he went.

Next morning Cabinet boxes half filled his room.

In those days Cabinet Ministers did not discuss Cabinet questions with women in the hearing of servants, and Cabinet secrets were secrets, and we, figuratively speaking, double-locked the door and pulled down the blinds before proceeding with due solemnity to open boxes.

Inside one was half a sheet of notepaper from Lord Granville, known to his colleagues as Pussy.

So far as I could judge, Granville's great value

rested on his marked ability to shepherd back to the fold recalcitrant Cabinet Ministers.

On the sheet of paper was written:

"DEAR H.,—I still disagree with you, but to prove my absolute confidence in your judgment I hereby authorise you to invest £10 for me at Newmarket.—G."

I became deeply attached to Lord Hartington.

He was abnormally shy and very reserved, but he had a heart of gold.

I once knew him take a very early train to Newmarket—a terrible ordeal for one who usually got up at midday—solely to help a young stable lad who had appealed to him to get him out of some trouble.

I believe I once had a unique experience.

I once saw Lord Hartington cry. It was when he first heard of Gordon's death.

He threw himself into an armchair and gave a great sob. Tears coursed down his cheeks, and it is characteristic of the man that he made little attempt to disguise his emotion and none to wipe his face.

I seem to have drifted from India back to my old War Office haunts.

Forgive me.

LETTER XVI.—ASSAM AND RHINOCEROS

SIMLA, *April 30th*, 1911.

WHEN I left England I made up my mind to shoot at least one of every kind of the dangerous wild-beast family in India. I was warned by those who were conversant with India and its game that I should almost certainly fail to carry out my undertaking; but that there was every likelihood that I should get soaked with malaria, not improbably be hurt, and that I might, as a special favour, get killed.

My age and the great burden of my work, with its consequential difficulty of absence from the seat of government, added materially to the weight of my self-imposed task. None the less, in two years and a half I have managed to shoot, in some cases alone and on foot, at least one, and in some cases three or four specimens, of every kind of Indian big game with one exception, that exception being a rhinoceros.

Just as "everyone" had told me it was out of the question for a lame old man to get a bison, so "everyone" assured me that it was even more out of the question for the same to get a rhinoceros. Having got a bison, I discounted the "out of the question" contention and made up my mind to shoot a rhinoceros.

The said beast is getting very scarce in India.

Some are left in Burmah and a few are to be found in Assam, where efforts are being made to get them to multiply in sanctuaries.

There is difficulty in obtaining permission to shoot near the reserved forest, and everywhere it is very difficult to approach a rhinoceros in India.

So far as I can make out, it is ever a "stern chase." You get on the track of a rhino, follow the trail almost day and night *à la* "Trail of the Yellow-stone Stag," and if you can last as long as or longer than the rhino you may get a shot at him. He lives in swampy grass jungle, moving about not like an elephant on paths made by crushing down the reeds, but in tunnels bored through them.

The "grass" is from 12 to 20 feet high, and rhinos burrow through it as a mole does under the ground. These tunnels are very noticeable, but their ramifications render it impossible to follow them on foot. They form a labyrinth. Indeed, the daily occupation of a rhino seems to be to cross and twist and double in every direction except in a straight line towards the spot he is making for, generally a very muddy "wallow."

As a consequence tracking the Indian rhino is an excessively difficult operation, and even the best of trackers are constantly at fault and have to retrace their steps or "cast round" in the hope of restriking the trail.

Thanks to the kindness of the Provincial Government of Eastern Bengal and Assam, and to the assistance rendered by the local Government officials, I was able to arrange a shoot in a pestilentially malarial district of Assam in the hope of getting a rhino.

I left Calcutta on March 31st, 1911, and reached the Ganges ferry at Raita Ghat the same evening. Here I was held up for two days owing to delay in obtaining pad elephants.

I took the opportunity of looking at the Sara bridge works where a railway bridge is eventually to link up Bengal with Assam. It seemed to me to be a very arduous undertaking owing to the constantly changing nature of the river-bed, but no doubt the difficulty will be surmounted. The heat was intense.

Raita Ghat seemed to me very typical of the British occupation. Twice a day the mail (to and from Calcutta) arrives. The station-master fumes, the guard curses, the coolies groan or squabble, the passengers rush for the boat or train, and the luggage does its best to travel in the wrong direction. All is bustle and confusion, but some one English official (as often as not an ex-N.C.O.), by the plentiful use of the two words " carmine " and " blighter," evolves order out of chaos and all goes well.

The moment the boat and train are gone, all relapses into the typical India by the Ganges. A brown sad-faced woman fills a *garah* with water; just above her a buffalo wallows; just below her a man washes exceedingly foul linen. In mid-stream a native boat with a very white sail goes dreamily with the stream. A red mange-covered pye-dog licks a huge sore and a miserably thin calf eats sand, no doubt convinced that it is grass. All animals seem to be Christian Scientists in India.

Should we ever leave India *horresco referens*, would India relapse in one or two generations into the typical "India by the Ganges"?

And if the relapse came about, would the boatmen be less happy, and could the woman and the dog and the calf be more miserable, than at present? And would the strong but rare English official flourish elsewhere and stupidly, illogically, unimaginatively turn bad into good with the aid of "carmine" and "blighter"?

After crossing the Ganges I rejoined the train and at 10 next morning "descended" at a small station in a fever-stricken spot in the jungle. I was met by the Deputy-Commissioner, who drove me some twenty-six miles through wild, I might almost say savage, country to a forest bungalow (where I met the Deputy-Conservator), and which was to be my first camp. They were both most kind to me, and took an infinity of trouble to get me my rhinoceros.

Next day we moved some fifteen miles farther inland and camped almost at the foot of the Himalayas south-east of Bhootan, and, I fancy, not very many marches from where the Abors give trouble.

The next morning, April 8th, I was on my elephant, as usual, at 4 a.m. We got to our ground at dawn, but the trackers made a bad mistake. They "crossed" a fresh trail without detecting it. This resulted in six hours' hard work merely to get back to the very spot where we had "missed" and starting *de novo* on a six-hour-old trail. On the whole, however, the tracking was very, very good and intensely interesting. About

1 o'clock, after many disappointments, I was raced up a "very hot" trail, and I got a glimpse of a disappearing rhino-back 60 yards off in the grass. I put my bullet into the withers and the rhino fell, practically dead in his tracks.

The rhino stood 5 feet 6½ inches at the shoulder, but the horn was very much worn and consequently very short.

I returned to camp elated but worn out; too weary to eat, drink, smoke or sleep, with neuritis gnawing at me like a ravening wolf.

On the following day we returned to our first camp, avoiding a mud road where a rogue elephant was holding up all wayfarers.

During our rhino-tracking we came across a fine python, an amiable reptile who moved quietly out of our way.

On the 11th I started for the railway, which I reached after a fourteen hours' journey, slept that night in a rest bungalow, and next morning parted with the Deputy-Commissioner, to whom I was greatly indebted, and reached Gauhati on the 12th.

Whilst waiting at Gauhati I came across a belated vernacular paper which informed me that the Viceroy was going to Dehra Dun, "where there will be some cheerful talking." This sounded very much as though His Excellency proposed to read the Riot Act. I afterwards ascertained that "cheerful talking" was native printerese for "cheetal stalking."

Assam reminded me in part of the Nepal Terai and partly of Southern India. It is very green and should be very fertile, but it is horribly unhealthy in parts, and the fever-stricken inhabitants reminded me of the Maremma folk of old days.

The population seems to be a collection of various races, chiefly Mongolian: the Mech, the Rabha, the Kachari, and the Garos—all very wild-looking and mostly somewhat yellow; but there are also considerable numbers of Santhals, who come from the Nagpur districts and who are quite black.

The province generally appeared to me to have been administratively neglected, and the executive staff seemed to be overworked and somewhat discouraged.

The weather on the whole was fair. Brilliant and intensely hot sun one day. Cloudy and almost chilly another day, with violent, pitiless hail-storms thrown in.

The Brahmaputra is a beautiful river, the banks where I was being rocky, often high, and covered with trees and shrubs of the brightest green. Some of the bends of the river are not unlike narrow bits of a Swiss lake. I have enjoyed it all intensely, but I have contracted a severe attack of malignant tertiary fever.

LETTER XVII.—GOVERNMENT OF INDIA, SIMLA, AND I.C.S.

CALCUTTA, *February 5th*, 1912.

I HAVE just returned from a week's visit to Rangoon and find your letter in which you ask me "what the Government of India is like." The Government of India is like but one thing else in the world, and that is the Government of the Church of Rome. The Viceroy is a sort of Pope, a mixture of regal and law-giving holiest of the holy; but the real ruler of India is the Secretary of State—the prototype of the Secretary of the Propaganda. Then come the Cardinals—that is to say, the Members of Council. The latter, like the former, may be divided into three classes: the indifferent, the acquiescent, and the militant. A strong Viceroy gathers his Council together, makes the best of what is best in it, and if his tenure synchronises with that of a pliant Secretary of State, governs India, just as occasionally a Pope has governed the Church of Rome. If, however, a Viceroy is a weak specimen of humanity and his tenure synchronises with that of a masterful Secretary of State, the whole Government is centred in the Secretary of the Propaganda.

Wholesale changes in the position of the Viceroy will in time become inevitable, but so long as the present dispensation obtains, to the Indian the Viceroy is the personification of power and majesty, the dispenser of favours and the upholder of justice. Everything centres in that one man, and every time that one man is overruled, English rule receives a serious set-back. If a Viceroy is a capable, strong man, is well in touch with English opinion and English politics, and if he takes his Council into his confidence and has their support, he will very rarely find himself in conflict with the English Government. But if, on the contrary, he is out of touch with English public opinion and is entirely in the hands of his bureaucracy, he is likely to assume an attitude from which he may be obliged to recede, and every time he does so, the position of England in India is weakened.

Many of our Indian difficulties are attributable to the marvellous system under which for some six months of each year the Government of India goes to sleep—and does so on the top of a mountain seven to eight thousand feet high. There the Government devotes itself to a mild form of seaside holiday. It is entirely out of touch with India, and especially out of touch with the English commercial and industrial communities. But sedition, unrest, and even murder may have been going on elsewhere none the less. Up at Simla the news of an outrage is received with languid and transient interest. The burning questions are polo finals or racing, with the all-absorbing tennis tournaments to fill up voids in the daily life; consistent and sustained policy is apt to disappear at Simla.

From the placidity of Simla the Government suddenly finds itself for the other six months of the year thrust into a vortex of political excitement and ferment. What at Simla would be regarded as a "tiresome incident" becomes in Calcutta a "formidable danger," and the Government feels impelled to do something and to do that something in a hurry. A "strong policy" must be adopted; "repression" is spoken of in lieu of "sympathy," and "hitting back hard" instead of "brotherly hand-shaking" becomes the order of the day.

These rapid and emotional transitions and the protean changes of policy which usually follow are not good for British rule in India.

The day, the inevitable day, will come when India will have earned and attained self-government, and then her present difficulties will disappear. Meanwhile, however, we can justly claim that the Government machine is working, and working very fairly well. *E pur si muove!* and if we do, it is thanks to the most extraordinary and in some respects wholly admirable machinery evolved by the mind of man. The most remarkable machinery the world has ever seen, not excepting that which enabled the Roman Empire to hold its colonies—the Indian Civil Service. It is a living testimony to the stability and love of justice inherent in the English race. It would be presumptuous for me to criticise; it is almost presumption on my part to express admiration for a Service which is unique, which has made India what it is, and which I have blind confidence will help to make India what it should and will be—

the most marvellous, the most prosperous, and, not impossibly, the most high-minded Empire of the world.

My debt of gratitude to the Civil Service of India is not only personal, it is immeasurable.

I recognise somewhat sadly that I am not at all a *persona grata* to the great majority of Indian Civil Servants. My policy has perforce been a policy of retrenchment, and I question whether any Finance Minister anywhere can be popular if he does his duty without fear or favour. He must, in fact, be an animated negative, and however successful his administration may prove the noes are numerous and ever remembered, whilst the yesses, *rari nantes in gurgite vasto*, are soon forgotten. Sir Michael Hicks-Beach was perhaps one of England's best Finance Ministers, but I have yet to learn that he revelled in popularity when Chancellor of the Exchequer. Of a Finance Minister beloved by all I should be disposed to say, *Timeo Chancellor et dona ferentem.* So few gifts have I had to bestow that I have earned the sobriquet of " Not a bob !"

Unpopular though I may be with the Civil Service, they have, I hope and think, accorded me their respect, and most assuredly have they lavished on me supreme loyalty, ready and invaluable assistance. Not once has any one of them tried to trip me up. Rather have they helped me over many a stile. What perhaps has touched me most has been the keen, unselfish and unjealous manner in which they have, when opportunity offered, helped me in shikar. More cannot be said.

The Civil Servants of India have a cruel lesson yet to learn. It is the lesson taught the Civil Service of England by Mr. Gladstone. They have to learn that the public servant is the servant of the public, and it will be a distasteful lesson. But they will be the better for it and will emerge from the transformation better officials, better citizens, and in all respects bigger men individually and collectively. I believe that before many years have elapsed they will have to face far-reaching and distasteful changes, but that they will survive the ordeal, and with honour, I am as confident as I am of anything. As India advances so will they advance with advantage to the country and credit to their service.

LETTER XVIII.—UNITED PROVINCES TERAI TIGERS AND SIR JOHN HEWETT

SIMLA, *April 28th*, 1912.

SHOOTING at tigers from a howdah has never appealed to me. I write "shooting at" advisedly, for it is rare to get a tiger to oneself when shooting from an elephant. It generally means several people firing at the same beast at the same moment. Besides, it is a shocking waste of tigers, just as a deer drive in Scotland is a shocking waste of stags. But my chief objection to shooting from elephants is that the real joy of tiger-shooting is absent. There is so little "even odds" about it. Someone has said that it is as safe as shooting a mad dog from the top of an omnibus. I will not go so far as that, but danger is certainly reduced to a minimum.

For me one of the great charms of big-game shooting in India lies in being more or less alone in the jungle, awaiting the early dawn when man awakes and the jungle goes to sleep, when the golden sun of India begins to radiate warmth and glorious colouring. The noontide rest in the shade, preferably in solitude and well away from "the loud laugh that speaks the vacant mind," the joyful awakening of the jungle at sunset and the awe-inspiring, unexplainable noises of the jungle at night—all are practically denied to one in a camp peopled by scores, possibly by hundreds, and surrounded by many of the comforts and some of the luxuries of so-called civilisation. Elephants mean a big *bandobast*, and often what I detest above all things (and quite as much in England as elsewhere)—"women out shooting."

Accordingly I have up to now refused the kind invitations which I have received to shoot off elephants.

But I gratefully accepted John Hewett's invitation to join him in his United Provinces Terai shoot, first because his *bandobasts* are, I had always been given to understand, absolutely perfect, and chiefly because I like and admire both him and his wife.

Like all strong, capable men, "Jack" Hewett doubtless has his enemies, and I have heard it said that he has at times been administratively unconventional.

In my somewhat exceptional experience of men, I have rarely, very rarely, met a really clever man who was either unscrupulous or untruthful. Putting aside the ethical consideration, tortuous methods "do not pay." Truth and straight dealing are really the weapons on which a clever man relies, and Hewett is undeniably a very clever man. He certainly is a marvellously successful Lieutenant-Governor, and his administration of the United Provinces of Agra and Oude reflect as much credit on English rule as on himself.

All of which means that on March 29th I started for Lucknow anticipating a delightful and somewhat novel experience, and my anticipations have been amply fulfilled.

On Sunday, March 31st, at 8 a.m. we reached our first camp at Chiriyaehang, having travelled by a narrow-gauge railway to within three miles of the camp.

Our party consisted of the Lieutenant-Governor, Lady Hewett, and Miss Lorna Hewett; Lieutenant-Colonel R. F. C. Gordon, Private Secretary to the Lieutenant-Governor; Lieutenant R. V. Pollock, A.D.C. to the Lieutenant-Governor; J. V. Collier, Assistant Conservator of Forests; Thomas Carr, Deputy-Conservator of Forests; and Major P. H. Clutterbuck, Conservator of Forests, Naini Tal.

Gordon, a man of much charm, left no stone unturned to make me happy and comfortable. The last, admittedly quite the finest organiser of "on-elephant" tiger shoots in India, also a really first-class Forest officer. The other three were very pleasant men, who went out of their way to show me every kindness and consideration.

The guests in addition to myself consisted of young Atkinson, Captain of the Viceroy's Body-guard, singularly good-looking and attractive; Sir Henry Richards, Chief Justice; and Ludovic Porter, of the United Provinces Civil Service—beloved of all, including the wild bees, who invariably settled on him, greatly to his discomfort and disfigurement.

In the afternoon of April 1st we had a march round in long grass after leopard, getting one.

On Tuesday we moved camp and shot *en route* a large hornless sambhar for food.

At one point very near the road a leopard watched us quite unconcernedly although our party consisted of twelve elephants and a crowd of "retainers."

We reached Dogari Camp late, after an intensely hot and tiring march.

On Wednesday we had a big tiger drive and a very unlucky one. We saw four tigers but only one, a *batcha*, was shot, by Gordon.

Although tiring, these moves from camp to camp are full of interest. The country is somewhat unlike any other part of India which I have been in and the people seem different to the Indians of elsewhere. The whole produces a curious sense of expanse and originality.

During our peregrinations I saw for the first time what I can only describe as a rookery of vultures. They had built their nests in a clump of large high trees, and were cawing and feeding their young just like rooks. The stench from the "rookery" was quite unbearable at close quarters, and most disagreeable even a long way off, when carried by the wind. I was told that vultures not infrequently build in the vicinity of a burial-ground. They had done so in this instance.

This district for a considerable portion of the year is very unhealthy, cholera, the plague, and smallpox being prevalent. The sanitary administration seems sound enough, but it is heavily handicapped by the prevailing (illegal but irradicable) practice indulged in by the natives of burying those who die of the diseases I have enumerated in the dry sand-banks in the river-beds. They believe that the flood in the rainy season will wash away contagion. So it may, but only very much to the detriment of those down-stream. The water-borne infection is thus spread. I have not come across this practice anywhere else.

On the 4th we made a large dĕtour in the hope of driving in tiger, but only put up two owls!

A small elephant carrying soda-water almost trod on a half-grown tiger and appeared to go clean mad from fright. I understand there was a slump in soda-water; but it all happened behind our shooting-line.

On the 5th Miss Hewett shared a fine tigress with Collier. It was the only one we saw.

On the 6th we reached Sarket Camp, where we had a long hot chase and killed a magnificent 10-foot 4-inch tiger. He fell to Gordon's rifle.

Next day, Sunday, we rested and worshipped in a temple not built with hands.

Monday proved a blank day.

On Tuesday I tried alone for a swamp deer, but failed to find one.

On Wednesday at Horaï we went after tiger. A very good one was moved. He was coming straight to me, when a jumpy native turned him and he fell to Richards' shot.

On Friday we moved to Unchagaon Camp. Next day was the red-letter day of the expedition and a lucky day for me. Very early in the morning the invaluable and untirable Clutterbuck had started with a very large number of elephants to beat in a huge crescent-shape formation a great extent, many miles in fact, of jungle. He gradually narrowed his front, thus driving whatever game was within the semicircle of elephants into a patch of 6-foot grass about 3 acres in extent.

The whole thing was admirably timed. We had just finished luncheon when Clutterbuck wheeled us into line. I think the elephants numbered between sixty and seventy. They were ranged in crescent formation close beside each other, their flanks actually touching. The elephants bearing the "guns" were placed at intervals in the line, and slowly and silently we closed in on the centre of the grass patch. It contained no less than four tigers, all of which were eventually killed.

The space between the points of the two horns of the crescent of elephants opened on to a stretch of bare ground left purposely at the disposal of the tigers. But the tigers knew well enough that to cross that bare ground spelt certain death, and for quite a quarter of an hour they treated us to a sight never to be forgotten.

Repeatedly they charged the line of elephants only to fall back before a *chevaux de frise* of tusks. Roaring and beside themselves with fear and fury, they repeatedly sprang, goat-like, straight into the air. Each time they did so they presented a fair target and were freely shot at.

So far as I was able to judge, Lady Hewett accounted for one "on her own," and later on one fell to my shot.

I had been placed at the point of one of the crescent horns, and quite at the last one tiger, the largest, broke out just in front of me and bounded up a bank which flanked my side of the grass patch. I fired, and the tiger came slipping down the bank and lay dead at the foot of it. Atkinson, who was not far from me, also fired, but he insisted that it was I who had killed the tiger, and an examination of the body showed him to be right.

Thus ended what a stalker would have termed a "graaand day."

Of its kind the whole expedition was a masterpiece.

A dynamo on bullock carts provided us with electric light in camp. The food and drink were superlatively good. Everything possible was done to ensure comfort. Nothing was forgotten or mismanaged and our time-table was fulfilled with a punctuality unknown on any railway system. Also the sporting arrangements were perfection.

It was an experience at once delightful and unique, but it is one I should not care to repeat.

I think what I enjoyed as much as anything were the long quiet evenings after dinner in Hewett's tent. What he does not know about India is not worth knowing, and from an educational standpoint alone I have greatly benefited by my holiday.

On Saturday, April 13th, I left for and reached Bareilly, and the last two, subsequent, days I have devoted to selecting a house in Delhi for my last winter in India.

LETTER XIX.—KATHIAWAR LION AND SIR GEORGE CLARKE

DELHI, *May 2nd*, 1912.

No matter how many or how deadly be the sins committed by George Sydenham Clarke, otherwise His Excellency the Governor of Bombay, I feel confident that the Recording Angel will, for his superbenevolent treatment of me, wipe them all out and accord him the benefit of a clean slate.

To his kindness I owe the exceptional privilege of securing a very, very rare trophy—to wit, a maneless lion of India and an exceptionally fine one.

I am assured that not one had been shot for over thirty years, and on the last occasion the lion killed one of the then Governor's Staff. The fact is there are very few of them. Indeed, at one time only sixteen were believed to exist. They are to be found in only one spot in the whole continent, in the forest of Gir, and they are strictly preserved. It is only at rare intervals, generally when drought has killed off all the cattle, that one takes to man-killing, and then he has to be tried, condemned, and executed.

Of the lions of Gir an early Italian writer makes the quaint remark that they are like honest men and truthful women—"Esistono, ma rari."

Gir Forest is an extensive, sunbaked district

covered with bushes that resemble dried-up mimosa, very plentifully furnished with sharp thorns. Such trees as exist are few and far between.

It is owing to the lions having for centuries forced their way through this thorn-covered bush that their mane (incessantly torn off) has ceased to grow. I understand that there is a district in Africa where the lions carry little or no mane from the same cause.

It fell to my lot to be in India when a "criminal lion" came in evidence, and it was my good-fortune that my sojourn in the East synchronised with that of so sympathetic and generous-minded a Governor of Bombay.

I had always longed to complete my list of the big game of India, but I had given up all hope of filling up the lion gap, when Sir George one day said to me: "I can and will give you what no one else in the world can give you—a Kathiawar lion." And he kept his word.

On April 15th I started for Kathiawar State, and I shall not easily forget the journey there and back.

It is not a season when sane people travel across the plains of India, and I had two Indian servants down with heat apoplexy on the return journey.

On the 16th I reached Viramgam and proceeded by narrow-gauge railway in the most terrific heat, passing Rajkot and through a badly famine-stricken district. The cattle seemed to have all died off and I believe the human mortality had been somewhat heavy.

Kathiawar, which once formed part of the old

kingdom of Guzerat, is a Native State in the Bombay Presidency on the Arabian Sea. Gir or Gier Forest is in the south-eastern extremity of the Peninsula of Kathiawar on the Bay of Cambay, opposite Diu Islands, which belong to Portugal, and from whence it is said a nice little smuggling trade is carried on.

When I increased the import duties it was remarked that a constant stream of women flowed up-country. They came under especial notice because they appeared to be in pain and seemed to walk with extreme difficulty. Investigation showed that their legs were absolutely covered with very thick rings of smuggled silver which in this fashion they carried into the interior. *Se non è vero, è ben trovato.*

On Wednesday, the 17th, I reached Verawal, where Robertson, the Resident, met me and drove me twenty-two miles to the camp at Kokhra. From first to last he devoted himself to making my expedition a success, and I shall always retain a vivid recollection of his unselfish kindness to me. We rode sixteen and walked two miles. Midway we were met by a deputation of the inhabitants. They gave me quite the most exquisite coffee I have ever tasted and a cordial welcome. They appeared to me to be as nearly as possible pure Arabs, and they had all the attributes of the Arab race: a fine physique, great dignity, marked courtesy, and much reserve. They are a fine, manly, independent people.

In overwhelming heat we had a lion drive. I saw no lion, but I was assured that one had been "moved."

This moving is a curious process.

A "kill" is watched, and when the gorged lion has eaten and drunk his fill his lying-up place is located and sufficient time is allowed to elapse to ensure his going off into a sound sleep.

In due course a number of men very silently creep as near as they dare to the lion's sleeping chamber, which they almost surround, leaving unguarded the line of retreat which it is considered the lion will probably take.

At a signal from the head shikari all the men give utterance in unison to an ear-splitting, demoniac yell which wakes up the lion under conditions calculated to make him about as ill-tempered as a retired Colonel of the old school with a severe attack of gout.

The men are careful not to show themselves, and are especially careful not to make the slightest noise. The head shikari allows about a minute to elapse and then gives the signal for yell number two.

The plan has never been known to fail. The lion thinks the whole performance uncanny and trots off or bounds away according to his temperament in the direction whence no sound has reached him, and if all goes well passes the spot where the sportsman has been posted—sometimes in a tree, sometimes behind one.

In this instance my post was beside a rock about the size and shape of a grand piano. But on this occasion no lion passed me. On the 18th and 19th, there being no news of lions, we stood at ease—ease which I very greatly needed. We were cheered by a visit from Mrs. Robertson, to whom I am greatly indebted for much trouble taken on my behalf, and who possesses the admirable qualities which characterise the Mufassal Englishwomen in India.

On the 20th we got *khabar* of a lion—a well-known, unusually big, old and grey lion—and started very early after him on foot. I think we were some ten hours following him. He at last lay up in a clump of bushes in a very small wood, almost the only wood I saw in Gir Forest. Gir Forest, like a Scotch forest, is treeless and equally bears its name on the *lucus a non lucendo* principle.

I was posted on rising ground behind a bulky tree-stump and the head shikari, a splendid specimen of the class, stood beside me. The "move" succeeded, but the lion did not wait for the second yell. Immediately he heard the first he bounded out and came past me at a hand-canter. He was inclining towards Robertson's post, when that kind, unselfish young man fired two shots over him, pushing him towards me. I hit the lion rather too high and too much behind to kill him straight away. He went a short distance and then lay up on a bare spot exactly in the attitude of the Nelson Monument lions, and we, the head shikari and myself, had to walk up to and finish him.

I fully expected him to charge us and confess to feeling at the moment in a "blue funk," but my shot had injured the spine and he could not rise, much less charge.

He was a grand beast, and when I looked at him lying dead, I confess that I would have given all

I have in the world to have been able to restore him to life.

He looked superb when he passed me, taking great leaps rather than galloping; he looked very formidable when sitting up wounded, and he looked noble in death. Of course, I am beyond measure delighted at getting a Gir lion, but the day is not far distant when I shall hate to kill any of God's creatures.

On the 21st I returned to Viramgam, and next day reached Delhi, a veritable wreck from intense heat and exhaustion. My damaged knee resembles a large and overripe pumpkin, and from my devoted personal assistant, Mr. Baker, I shall receive a well-merited rebuke.

LETTER XX.—FAUNA OF INDIA

SIMLA, *May 6th*, 1912.

I PROPOSE, *faute de mieux*, to offer you to-day a few remarks on some of the fauna of India.

I have the greatest regard for a tiger: I might almost say an affectionate regard. He is such a gentleman. A man-eater is said to be a cowardly brute who will sneak up to a wretched human unawares and kill and eat him. I have met but two man-eaters and they behaved as well as any other tiger.

A tiger only asks to be let alone. He takes toll of cattle from the ryots (peasants), but he more than recoups them their loss. The real enemies of the ryot are the wild-hog and the smaller deer. Both do an incalculable amount of damage to crops. Neither can be exterminated, and the numbers of each are greatly curtailed by tigers. Indeed, in localities where deer are very plentiful or where pig swarm, the loss in cattle from tigers is quite insignificant. Besides, it is usually an old and often diseased cow or a worthless young calf who gets killed through lagging behind or getting lost in the jungle.

Even when wounded a tiger will generally leave you alone if you are not quite close to him and give him a clear course. I never heard of a wounded tiger deliberately following a man or lying in wait for him as wounded buffalo and leopard almost invariably do. I never could look at a dead tiger without feeling a pang of genuine remorse, and the sight of one either prowling noiselessly through the jungle or charging is the most superb sight I have ever had the good fortune to witness. No doubt a tiger which has been wounded and has recovered is often a dangerous neighbour, but as a rule the natives do not seem to dread an unwounded tiger in the least.

I once saw a tiger break out from the side of a jungle which was being beaten towards me and trot across an open field in which a number of cattle were grazing, and in which the whole of the villagers were standing "looking at the gentlemen shooting"—just as villagers do at home when a covert is being driven for pheasants. He just trotted through the lot and hurt no one. Personally I would rather be in a field under like conditions than in a field at Home when some of my acquaintances had guns in their hands. I believe the risk at Home would be the greater.

On the other hand, leopards really are the enemies of the human race. I do not blame them for it. They kill many natives in the course of the year and eat a good many goats, but even leopards have their uses. They keep down the number of pye dogs (pariahs)—miserable, mangy, rabies-spreading curs, who but for disease, leopards, and muggers (crocodiles), would crowd out everything else.

I should rather have to deal with two tigers than one panther. A tiger cannot, at any rate does not, climb a tree; a leopard can and will.

A leopard will walk into a village at night, enter a hut and kill a sleeping native. I never heard of a tiger doing it. A wounded leopard will deliberately hide in a side-track or behind a rock and pounce on you when you are following him, and buffalo and bison will ring round you and charge you from behind in similar circumstances. A wounded tiger will retreat to the thickest jungle, and unless you go really close up to him, will hardly ever attack you gratuitously, so to speak.

I am fond of all animals and often think I shall give up shooting because of the genuine remorse I feel when I look at a dead animal whose life I have cut short. In Scotland I have often had to turn away from a dead red stag, and have thereby earned the contempt of the stalker, who has suspected me of not appreciating the strong "grând smull" of a dead stag. And it is with a big, big lump in my throat that I have turned away. I have not infrequently let off an animal in India because it was looking at me enquiringly, and I am not ashamed to own to it. I have often done the same with rabbits at Home. On the other hand, I never spare a snake or a mugger. I hate and fear both. They are, if you like, really detestable. The number of natives killed by snakes is proverbially large, but the number killed by muggers, is not, I suspect, much smaller. I suppose muggers are useful as water-scavengers, but why snakes were created I never could understand. Possibly, like Topsy, they grew, and Providence may have tolerated them much in the same way that Society puts up with scurrilous newspapers.

Scientists draw an absurd distinction between venomous and harmless snakes. As the American said of Red Indians, there is but one harmless snake and that is a dead one.

Bears are most amusing to watch but dangerous to meddle with. Natives are very frequently injured by bears and detest them. I once watched a bear up a tree trying to get at a honeycomb. The way he grumbled and cursed *sotto voce* when a bee managed to sting his nose was extraordinarily funny. At last the bees got the better of him, and he reluctantly slithered down the tree and walked sulkily away grumbling, just as does an old City clerk if he finds no room in the City bus on a rainy morning. A bear possesses the combined charms of a sulky porter and a slow railway booking-clerk. Had I the option, however, of shooting two of the three, I should let off the bear.

I always found it excessively hard to hit a bear. He looks enormous, generally gives you a fair chance, and has less vitality than the cat tribe and the deer tribe, but he is all fur! The contrast between a skinned and an unskinned bear is almost ludicrous. The only thing at all like it from the standpoint of contrast is a grey owl, which is all feathers. One takes a steady shot at what ought to be the bear's heart and the bullet just cuts through a mass of long black fur. It is as difficult to locate a bear's heart as it is to locate some human brains. Parenthetically I may mention that a bear's paw baked in a clay jacket is quite good eating.

Mr. Pig I dare not mention. He is as sacred to the Anglo-Indian as he is unclean to the

Mahomedan. I am, alas! too old to pig-stick, and only a pig-sticker can presume to pass wild-pig under review. I have shot pig in non-pig-sticking districts, but I always felt as though I had shot a fox. A wild-boar is reputed to be the pluckiest thing living.

À propos of boars, did you ever hear Lord Bowen's definition of a bore ?—A wild prig.

The sagacity of the elephant is proverbial, but it is not generally known that it is so great as to enable him to discharge clerical duties:

"A Settlement Officer hired an elephant named Ram Parshad, for Rs. 40 monthly, to carry him over a country so intersected with streams that other means of conveyance were useless. But the Financial Codes know nothing of elephants, and Ram Parshad's hire would never have passed the audit. So the Settlement Officer appointed Ram Parshad as a clerk on Rs. 40 in a post that happened to be vacant, and Ram Parshad drew his pay without objection, and no doubt earned it at least as well as his brother clerks."

The only large stags with which I am acquainted are the barasingha (which means, I believe, twelve points), a big animal with a fine head of from eight to fourteen points; the sambhar, also a fine stag with a good head of usually four to six points; and the swamp-deer, whose body is large, but whose head is relatively poor.

But no stag-shooting in India is, in my opinion, comparable with deer-stalking in Scotland. If I am told that I know very little about the former, my reply will be that with the exception of a few officers in British regiments, practically no one in India knows anything whatever about Scottish stalking.

The grandest dear in India is the Englishwoman of the Mufassal. There is nothing in the wide world to beat her. I allude especially to the wives of the junior officers of the various Government services.

Having often to live in a fever-stricken district, away from friends, tortured by heat, tormented by flies *et hoc genus omne*, dependent on very indifferent servants, for she can rarely afford to pay for good ones, with pining children and an overworked highly-strung husband, it would be no reflection on her if she gave the whole thing up as a bad job.

But she never flinches. Her own health, her ease and comfort, are her last consideration—her husband's health, comfort, and good repute her first.

And she never loses sight of her duty to maintain the *tenue* of an English lady.

I have often been intensely touched by the determination of the wife of some official with a very modest salary (and living is now *very* expensive in India) to make her somewhat dilapidated bungalow look like an English lady's home. The effort, no matter how hard, rarely, very rarely fails.

So long as England can produce such women the position of the Englishman in India is assured.

LETTER XXI.—SECOND DURBAR

DELHI, *December* 31*st*, 1912.

I REFRAINED from writing to you about the Great Delhi Durbar because I knew that the facile pens of the ready writers, the journalists, would furnish you with graphic and appealing accounts of that great event.

If I were asked what has made the most lasting impression on me, upon my word, I think it is the courage of which the Queen gave evidence when there was an alarm of fire at the Investiture. I do not care what may be said to the contrary, every man and woman, English and Indian, present winced—I can find no better expression—when the rumour ran that the huge *shamiana* was on fire; and no wonder, for had the fire taken hold of the gigantic beflagged and becurtained tent but few could have escaped.

One person only never winced—the Queen. My eyes were fixed on her face, and I can affirm that her eyelids never moved, and that her lips never twitched.

It was a remarkable exhibition of courage, dignity, and self-control.

Of the second Durbar (on December 23rd, 1912), I think I may be permitted to send you a very brief account, since regrettable circumstances obliged me greatly against my inclination to play the principal part in it.

I should explain that whilst the constitution of India provides for the death of a Viceroy, also for the insanity of a Viceroy, no provision is made to meet the case of a Viceroy otherwise rendered physically incapable of discharging the duties of his high office.

In cases of ordinary and temporary illness no great difficulty arises, as matters remain somnolescent pending his recovery; but where the disability is attributable to violence with the consequent risk of political disturbance, a locum tenens obviously becomes essential.

Under ordinary conditions the Senior Member of Council automatically becomes such substitute, but in a situation such as that created by the Delhi outrage rather more is wanted, as the burden of responsibility, power, and anxiety involved is a very grave one. The solution was found in the designation by the Viceroy of his *alter ego*.

I happen to be Senior Member of Council, and it was I whom Lord Hardinge, just before he lost consciousness, designated as his representative at the Durbar and until he could reassume his great position. Hence my appearance in the premier rôle.

Some of us doubted the expediency of holding a second Durbar. In the first place, the memory of the Great Durbar might possibly overshadow it to such an extent as to render it a ceremonial manqué. Secondly—and I felt this strongly—it was bound to cripple financially any minor State called upon to participate in it. Durbars drain the resources of Native States, and the response to the call for a display commensurate with the exceptional character of the King's Durbar had been so lavish that it seemed hardly considerate to call on Native States for a repetition thereof. However, Durbar number two was decided upon to the greater glory of "all and sundry," and every effort was made to ensure success.

Delhi is a town of broad streets where English houses are concerned, but not so in most of the Indian quarters, and owing to its peculiar character the Chandni Chowk, where the outrage occurred, is exceptionally narrow so far as the roadway is concerned. There is a locality in London which may be said to be almost a replica of the Chandni Chowk, and that is the Royal Avenue, Chelsea. Although the complete thoroughfare is very spacious, practically the whole of it is occupied by a gravelled centre space bordered by trees and with a narrow road on each side thereof.

The roads are on one side lined by a continuous row of houses in both Delhi and Chelsea, the difference being in the character of the houses in the two places.

In Chelsea the houses are of the ordinary London kind. In Delhi most of the houses are Indian with the usual covered balcony on each floor, the street floors being shops.

It will be evident that any elephant "processioners" perambulating along the narrow "border" street of the Chandni Chowk would be almost on a level with the first-floor balconies and immediately beneath the balconies of all the higher storeys.

Ceremonial processions in all countries involve

a certain amount of risk, and the East is no exception.

The route selected undoubtedly presented some elements of danger. To what extent warnings had been given to the Viceroy by those answerable for his safety I do not know, but whatever else, Hardinge is unquestionably a man of marked courage both physical and moral, and I question whether any scent of danger would have affected his decision. He wanted to "impress the native," as the saying is, and probably selected the route decided upon with that object in view.

Be that as it may, the selection turned out an unfortunate one, but I am bound to say that had it rested with me it is the selection I should myself have made.

The procession itself consisted of some fifteen huge state elephants smothered in paint and gilding and gorgeously caparisoned.

The howdahs also were elaborately decorated, that of the Viceroy being the much-talked-of silver howdah which Lord Curzon had built for himself for his Durbar.

His Excellency's elephant came first, then the Commander-in-Chief's, then mine. The elephants of the other members of Council followed in order of seniority, then that of the Lieutenant-Governor of the Punjab, and so on. The elephants, trunk to tail, almost touched. I was therefore able to witness closely exactly what occurred when the bomb was hurled at the Viceroy.

The procession had just passed the spot where a street called, I think, Esplanade Road opens on to the Chandni Chowk, when I saw something

(I could not distinguish what) thrown from one of the second-floor balconies in the direction of the first elephant. A thin blue-grey line of very fine smoke indicative of picric acid remained quite plainly visible on the line taken by the bomb from a balcony to across the road. I saw it quite clearly and am convinced for that reason that the missile was thrown from the second floor. The police think otherwise, but I am satisfied that I am right.

The bomb appears to have just missed Lord and Lady Hardinge, and to have landed in the second half, the back seat, of the howdah when it exploded. It killed the State Umbrella-bearer, wounded the attendant sitting beside him, and injured several people in the crowd.

I understand that Lady Hardinge turned to her husband and asked if he were hurt. He replied, "All right, go on." They were unaware of what had happened to their attendants.

The Viceregal elephant took no notice of the explosion, which was not a very loud one, and continued his stately progress, as did mine. The elephant of the Commander-in-Chief, however, swung round and got out of place; I thus got close up to the first elephant. At first I thought the Hardinges had both escaped injury, but I could see that the two men behind them had collapsed. The Viceroy sat bolt upright and gave no indication whatever of his hurt. All of a sudden, when we had gone about 30 yards from the spot where the outrage occurred, the tall, straight figure of the Viceroy literally crumpled up. Of course, his elephant was at once stopped, as were all the rest. Absolute quiet and perfect order prevailed. A ladder was placed against the side of the elephant, and Lady Hardinge, pale but quite cool and under perfect self-control, stepped quickly but calmly to the ground. In a firm, clear voice she ordered up the Viceregal motor-car and superintended the lowering of the body of her now unconscious husband. Her conduct throughout was that of a heroine—it is the correct term to use—and it enormously impressed all present.

As I have already said, before losing consciousness His Excellency designated me his *remplaçant*, and as soon as he had been taken away and his elephant moved to one side, I gave the order to proceed as though nothing had happened. The only change in regard to myself was that I found myself at the head of the procession instead of being number three, and that I held in my hand the manuscript notes of the Viceroy's speech to be delivered from the dais on which the peacock throne once stood, and which he had sent me, and which were bespattered with his blood.

The whole incident can be best described as shocking. It shocked rather than alarmed, leaving a feeling of stupefaction coupled with, I admit, a strong feeling of anger and resentment.

But what seemed to knock at one's heart was the magnificent bearing of Lady Hardinge.

From first to last that sweet woman was entirely self-possessed, and not for one moment did she fail to radiate confidence and inspire courage.

When the procession reached the entrance to the Naubat Khana we dismounted, and I received an address from the members of the Legislative

Council. In thanking them, I stated my conviction that a new era of happiness and prosperity was in store for India. I expressed my faith in India, her people, and her future, and said that I was absolutely certain that the tragic occurrence of that day would not cause the Government to falter in promoting under Divine guidance the best interests of the Indian people.

I then advanced and took my seat on the dais and held, what I know to have been, a most impressive Durbar in the historic Dewan-i-am.

Those present numbered over one thousand and were representative of all that is best in India. The sight was as gorgeous as it was impressive.

I prefaced the speech which Lord Hardinge was to have delivered, and which I read, by saying that I knew full well that every loyal Indian felt as great an abhorrence of the atrocious deed done that day as did every loyal Englishman; that Indian public opinion would be clear and emphatic in its condemnation of an outrage as senseless as it was iniquitous, and that all hearts, Indian and English alike, would go out to the Viceroy in his grievous pain and intense disappointment.

One had only to look at the faces of all the Indians present to see that I rightly gauged their feelings and correctly interpreted their mental attitude.

I concluded: "May the blessing of the Almighty ever guide and direct those who from this Imperial city shall govern this great Empire for the good of the people and their advancement in the path of progress and civilisation under the protecting ægis of the British Crown."

The Durbar was then closed with a blare of trumpets and a salute of thirty-one guns.

After the Durbar, and with the concurrence of my colleagues on the Council, I decided that the procession should return as had been arranged, passing through any native street which might lay on the route, and especially through the Chandni Chowk, the actual scene of the outrage.

Besides Lady Hardinge, only one other woman rode in the procession—Lady O'Moore Creagh. When the explosion occurred she remained on the elephant beside her husband, the Commander-in-Chief, entirely unaffected by it, and as cool and as collected as though nothing had happened. When Lady Hardinge left it would have been quite in the nature of things for her to have left also, but she declined to get out of the howdah, and sat through the long and trying march to the Fort, cheerful and smiling throughout, although, for all we knew, we might at any moment be treated to a shower of bombs. Her pluck has been greatly talked of amongst the Indian troops.

When the procession was about to start on the return journey, Lady Creagh was urged to drive straight home in her motor. She turned to me and said, "What do you say?" I replied, "Unless you are too tired I should get into the howdah again and show them what an Englishwoman is like." "That is just what I shall do," she said and did.

I confess that as we went past balcony after balcony full of, in many cases, rather low-class Indians, I could not help looking up at them and being filled with anxiety, not indeed on my own account, for I am a fatalist, but on account of the bright, dainty little lady on the Commander-in-Chief's elephant immediately behind me.

The two Durbars have brought prominently to the front, quite apart from their respective high positions, three women whose courage and the example they set should never be forgotten.

India is the land of intrigue, and women always have loved, do and ever will love, intrigue, and intrigue does not bring out the best side of their nature.

But India is also too often for Englishwomen the land of tragedy and of trial, and it is under the stress of tragedy and trial that their sterling qualities become so strikingly apparent.

From Home I am assured of reasonable freedom of action, confidence and support.

From my colleagues loyalty and co-operation.

No man could ask for more, and I am profoundly grateful.

Thus I find myself presiding at the Supreme Council, and am for the time being the representative of the Viceroy.

Unfortunately all this synchronises with the preparation of my last Budget.

The burden I bear is almost unduly heavy.

LETTER XXII.—PREFERENTIAL TARIFF

DELHI, *March 16th*, 1913.

PREPARE yourself for a rude shock, but prepare also for a rapid recovery, for this dry letter is meant not for you but for your brother, who takes a keen interest in the subject thereof, but whose present address I do not possess.

Chitnavis, who is a typical and very perfect specimen of a "Tory country squire," with his invariable courtesy, gave me private notice that he proposed to move in the Legislative Council a resolution in favour of a preferential tariff for India. The resolution reads as follows:

RESOLUTION TO BE MOVED BY SIR GANGADHAR CHITNAVIS.

That this Council recommends to the Governor-General in Council the desirability, in view of the loss of opium revenue, of considering financial measures for strengthening the resources of the Government, with special reference to the possibility of increasing the revenue under a system of preferential tariffs with the United Kingdom and the Colonies.

Eliminating the inevitable "beginning and ending," I shall endeavour to indicate the line I propose to take in dealing with the resolution.

Economic Relation of India to the Empire.

The striking feature of the present economic relations of India is the predominance of the United Kingdom over any other external country both in regard to import and export trade. Of the import trade of India the United Kingdom holds 49 out of 72 millions sterling. Of the export trade the United Kingdom holds 32 out of 123 millions. Fully half of the import trade consists of cotton piece goods from Lancashire. In regard to the other half of the import trade, the figures show that, so far, successful competition in India on the part of foreign countries has not been carried far.

Investments in India by external countries show a still greater British preponderance. According to the calculations of Sir George Paish, taking public issues only, the United Kingdom had no less than £365,400,000 invested in India and Ceylon, in 1910. To this must be added the large but undiscoverable figure of British money invested through private channels. No other country has financial interests in India at all comparable with those of the United Kingdom.

Indian native industries cover a wider field than is generally supposed, but relative to the resources and population of India they are small in volume and have not in recent years shown much increase. If we take into account the slow rate at which economic changes take place, the greatness of the interests affected, and the political, financial, and constitutional relations between India and the United Kingdom, it is clear that the development of India in the future must be dependent on, and primarily affected by, the policy pursued by the British Empire as a whole and particularly by the United Kingdom.

But changes not dissimilar in character from those which may be observed in other parts of the British Empire have taken place in the last twenty-five years in the character and direction of Indian trade. Modern methods of production have extended throughout the world; not only Western countries like the United States and Germany, but the Far East and Japan have enormously increased their productive power, and external markets for their goods have become a vital necessity to the stability and progress of their trade. India has been not unaffected by this development. The preponderance of the United Kingdom in India, as in other parts of the Empire, is still great, but it is diminishing. In the last twenty-five years the share of the British Empire in the import trade of India has fallen from 91 to 70½ per cent., while the share of foreign countries, chiefly Germany, Belgium and Austria-Hungary, has increased from 9 to 29½ per cent. Moreover, the United Kingdom has ceased to be the chief external market for Indian products. The United Kingdom proportion has fallen in the same period while the proportion of foreign countries, chiefly Germany and the United States and France, has increased. Time has not admitted of my working out the percentages. Even if allowance is made for the growth of direct trade, by diversion from the United Kingdom to foreign countries in this period, this general statement is still true. On the figures, relating as they do to a considerable period of time, it may be assumed that the competition of foreign and Western countries for the Indian market will increase and that the proportions of trade will, under present conditions, show a steady movement in the direction indicated.

But there is one important factor to be considered in regard to India which is of nothing like the same importance in regard to any other market in the British Empire, and that is the development of Japan. Japan has entered fully into the economic methods of the West. The new Japanese tariff shows all the leading features of that fiscal policy which has been employed with such effect in the development of the trade and resources of Germany and of the United States and other Western countries. But Japan enters this new field of commercial statesmanship under conditions very different from those of the West in regard to her nearness to the Indian market, the quantity and cheapness of the labour she can employ, and the facility with which she can imitate the products which have hitherto found favour in Far Eastern markets and adapt her methods of production to their needs. Competition in the Far East itself for the Indian market is therefore certain to be of a very formidable character, and if China follows Japan in the adoption of Western economic methods, the effect on the balance and adjustment of Indian trade might be incalculably great.

So far I have been stating facts which are accessible to any student of contemporary economics and I have refrained from drawing any inferences from them whatsoever. But I have no wish to shut my eyes to the irresistible inference which they arouse in certain minds. The school of thought which regards the days of Free Trade as numbered would take my facts as clear evidence that the duty of India, as part of the British Empire, is to build up for itself a tariff wall which will check those threatened diversions of our trade. If Germany and the United States, they will say, have already seized, and if Japan and China are going to seize, upon an ever-increasing share in our trade, is it not our obvious duty to readjust our schedule of import customs in such a manner as will check those tendencies and place our market more freely, instead of less freely, at the disposal of our own Empire? Incidentally, they add, will not arrangements of this nature operate to protect and foster the nascent industries of India?

PROTECTION.

The Indian Protectionist movement has undoubtedly, to a certain extent, been encouraged by the agitation in favour of Protection which has for some years been carried on—so far without practical success—by a section of the community in the United Kingdom. With that great controversy in its broader aspects it is not my place or my intention to deal. But we must remember that the agitation for Protection is linked with a policy of Imperial Preference; a matter which is of considerable interest to India.

I have been at some pains to discover the proposals advocated under the term Tariff Reform so far as they concern the trade relations of the Mother Country with India. So far as I have been able to learn, the references to this subject have been as yet too vague and indecisive for much to be deduced from them.

The "Speakers' Handbook" of the Tariff Reform League propounds preferential proposals with regard to India in a paragraph (page 185) which, whatever other opinions may be expressed about them, is certainly concise and intelligible. It is as follows:

> "Preference would mean to India that the United Kingdom and the Colonies would give freer entry to Indian tea, coffee, sugar, wheat, and all Indian staple products, and it would mean to us that the Indian import duty on a large number of British manufactures would be either abolished or reduced."

I make no comment upon it, except to invite attention to the last portion of it, which must be of intense interest to all; and especially to those who are imbued with the spirit of Protection for our industries.

The broad question of whether Protection would work to the general economic advantage of India or not is deserving of careful consideration, as the issue may at some future time be forced to the forefront.

One object of tariff Protection is presumably the "encouragement" of domestic industry, and it is effected by the imposition of Customs duties on imported goods for the express purpose of prohibiting, or at any rate restricting, the imports of such goods as are similar to, or may be substituted for, goods manufactured or produced in a given country.

The means whereby Protection works, and the method in which it is intended to work, is by raising Home prices. If you do not raise Home prices as a result of restricting foreign competition, you can hardly "encourage" industry; if you succeed in "encouraging" industry by a tariff, it can only, I think, be by raising Home prices. That is an axiom on which all economists appear to be agreed.

Now any such artificial increase in Home prices which Protection ensures, and by which it operates, may lay a grievous burden on the shoulders of our population. In some countries where Protection has been established the evils of this inevitable result have indeed been mitigated by natural or artificial circumstances unconnected with tariffs. Thus the natural wealth and vast mineral and agricultural productiveness of the United States, and the inventiveness and energy of their inhabitants, have enabled them for many years to bear a tariff burden under which other communities must have succumbed. The energy, thrift, and enterprise of the population of Germany, and the rigid discipline under which they are schooled, have had a somewhat similar result in that country. But even in Germany and America the revolt against Protection has been growing in recent years, and appears to incline towards a movement away from Protection.

I mentioned these instances to show that the introduction of Protection into a country is not universally and necessarily followed by disaster. But the natural and economic conditions which prevail in India are what we have to consider. In other words, what results would Protection produce for her? We have here an enormous population of the very poor; and however limited their physical requirements may be, the cheapness of the things they need is essential to their very existence. Can it be denied that artificially-produced dearness would be injurious to the well-being of a great majority of the people of this country? And if we are told that Protection will increase wages so as to compensate the wage-earner for the rise in prices, we must remember that by far the largest proportion of the working Indian population is engaged in agriculture.

Assuming that Protection would lead to a general increase in the wages of our manufacturing industries, what would be the effect on the rest of the population, who are to a large extent merely consumers? Where are the increased wages to come from which are to enable them to face with equanimity any artificial increase in the cost of living?

Agriculture is not in the main, so far as I understand the Protectionists' arguments, one of the industries which a tariff wall would assist in India; and consequently the rise in wages of the manufacturing classes would not extend *ipso facto* to the rural classes. Very possibly the general operation of economic laws would tend to pull up the remuneration of the latter in time; but especially in a conservative country like India the process would be slow and gradual; and in the interval an immense amount of hardship and suffering might be imposed on the great body of our Indian workers. A time of transition is always painful; and in this case it would also be protracted.

Protection attempts to apply State direction to production. It diverts trade from what may be called its natural channel into an artificial channel. It is often held that if by Protection an old industry is encouraged or a new industry created in a given country, that result is a clear indication of an increase in national wealth. But any such gain may be outweighed by a loss. The industry so artificially created or encouraged has been likened to a pauper. It cannot continue to exist unless it continues to receive dole after dole, and thus it lays a lasting burden on the general consumer, and through him on the economic growth of the State.

Economists have always been inclined to admit, to a limited degree, the efficacy of what is known as the "infant industry" argument, as used by List, Mill, and others, and which is adopted in an exaggerated form by some Indian Protectionists. It is based on the theory that if the failure to establish an industry in a given country on a sound basis is due merely to lack of skill, or to some other obstacle which technically might be surmounted if that industry were granted temporary tariff Protection, it might be advisable to grant it Protection. Economists hold that such Protection would indeed inflict a burden on the community by raising the prices of necessaries, but argue that if the industry in question should, after a limited number of years, be sufficiently firmly established to be able to exist without a tariff in the face of foreign competition, the resultant gain might counterbalance or even exceed the initial loss.

Can the advocates of Protection in India satisfy the legislature that, under a protective tariff, it will be possible to establish industries in this country which will eventually be able to fulfil the conditions thus laid down as a test of success? Do you believe that, with—I quote from Mill—"a moderate Protecting duty granted for a certain limited number of years—say, ten, or at the very most, twenty, during the latter part of which the duty should be on a gradually diminishing scale, and at the end of which it should expire," you can build up industries in India? Can you assure those responsible for the Government of India that these industries "will be able to produce articles as cheap as, or cheaper than, the price at which they can be imported" under a limited Protective system? Unless you are in a position to demonstrate these important points, the case for tariff Protection is on unsound ground.

Foreign competition, unimpeded by Protection, may have acted as a stimulus to industry, necessitating enterprise, inventiveness, economy, and efficiency in production to a high degree. It has not had that effect to any appreciable extent in India; but until our endeavours to improve our industrial methods and organisation in general have hopelessly failed, we can hardly call on the State to assist us by protecting our industries at the cost of the enormous number of our very poor consumers.

I have now stated a number of the chief arguments for and against Protection as an abstract theory. I am conscious that I may have stated them with somewhat more insistence on the objections than on the arguments in favour of the theory; but the reason for my doing so is that, if I may say so, the arguments making for Protection are more prominent in the mind of Indian publicists than those which are hostile to it, and, although I am very far from suggesting that this Council approaches the subject with a bias in favour of Protection, I am anxious that they should clearly realise the facts which India would have to face if such a policy were ultimately adopted. On the other hand, I have refrained from touching upon some of the most powerful reasons that ought to make a country hesitate before embarking on a Protectionist policy. For example, I have not attempted to allude to the financial aspects of Protection. That branch of the subject would require a very lengthy explanation. It would have to take cognisance of the great alteration which a tariff wall in India would effect in the balance of our trade, in the arrangements that now exist for the payment of our external debt, and in the whole of our exchange policy. This aspect of the question is one of extraordinary complexity, as well as of no small speculation; and I need hardly say that it would have to be most exhaustively considered before any steps could be taken towards Tariff Reform. I have avoided any reference to the ethical aspects of Protection as a State policy, but I would earnestly ask all to study the inner history of the influence of Protection upon political morality in the countries where it has been established for any length of time, and to consider with care whether the risks which other countries have experienced would be a fair burden to throw upon the awakening political life of India.

INDIA WITHIN THE EMPIRE.

I come now to the next natural division of my subject, which arises from the consideration that India is part of the British Empire, and that its interests and its wishes cannot be ignored in any movements which affect the policy of the Empire in relation to international trade. The cardinal feature of this consideration is the fact that India has already a tariff and that its tariff, although the rates have varied considerably from time to time and have in the past been materially higher than they are now, is essentially designed for the purposes of revenue and not with the view to Protection.

In these circumstances it is of the utmost consequence that those who are responsible for the economic future of India should consider carefully what position India is to occupy in regard to the British Empire policy. Looking at the facts of the case and the admissions of foreign writers and statesmen, there can be no doubt that the policy of free importation practised by the United Kingdom in regard to her own Home market has been of great advantage to countries like Germany and the United States in carrying out their own economic views, and in building up their own industries. But for the facility which British policy has created for the disposal of their surplus products the high tariff policy they have pursued would not have been attended with the success which they have actually enjoyed. The counterpart of that high tariff policy, pursued in exclusively national interests by foreign countries, has been the exploitation of such markets of the world as have been left open to their efforts.

In the British Empire, however, the United

Kingdom has for many years abandoned the exploitation of Colonial markets in the interest of the Mother Country and has left her self-governing Colonies free to do what her statesmen thought right in the interests of those Colonies, with the result that an Empire policy has grown up in the conditions so created different in character and in objects from any policy which the world has ever seen before, which has for its object the strengthening of the Empire as a whole by the development of the economic interests of its several parts, and the linking together of the Mother Country and the constituent States of the Empire by a co-ordination of policy and the intertwining of their economic interests by a system of preferences.

India, owing to special conditions, has not been brought into the general Imperial trade movement, but in view of the modification of the old ideas in regard to free importation and the economic principles underlying them, and the progress of events throughout the Empire in the last thirty years, it is conceivable that India may in the future be unable to maintain a policy of absolutely free importation under which she must suffer all the incidents of exploitation of her own market. Hence the key of the future policy of India must be found in observing what is the nature of the movement taking place in the rest of the British Empire, and in considering under what conditions India could fall in with any general policy of Empire preference.

Let us see what the progress of the Imperial movement has been. The Empire consists of self-governing Dominions, Crown Colonies, Dependencies, Protectorates, at every conceivable stage of economic development; but during the last twenty years, irrespective of Governments and party changes in the Mother Country, the measures adopted by, or in the interests of, different parts of the Empire show a steady and continuous movement in the direction of Empire trade consolidation. Canada adopted the policy of preference in 1897—that is, she gave special tariff concessions to the United Kingdom and to the Empire as a whole, and under the successive changes of the tariff, Canada and the rest of the Empire have been drawn together in ever closer relations. Canada was followed by New Zealand in 1903, South Africa in 1906, Australia in 1907. Furthermore a series of inter-Colonial preferential arrangements between Canada, New Zealand, Australia, and South Africa have been concluded, and to these has now been added an arrangement between Canada and the West Indies, which in some respects is more remarkable than any which have preceded it. Thus the self-governing portions of the British Empire excepting alone the United Kingdom and Newfoundland have gradually formed a network of Imperial and inter-Imperial preferential trading arrangements. The British Empire may be said to be regarded as consisting not of an aggregation of separate entities with no mutual relations to each other, but of a family of States animated by a common family purpose. Each State in the first instance organises its tariff and its policy to suit its own financial and economic needs and gives an Imperial sanction to its policy by granting to other parts of the Empire as large a measure of trade advantages over foreign countries as is consistent with its own economic development.

The preferences in the tariffs of the self-governing Dominions, while differing in detail, have certain general features in common. The tariffs have for their main objects the production of Government revenue, the protection of Home industries, the development of an export trade, and the encouragement of inter-Imperial trade. The tariffs therefore include—

(*a*) Duties imposed for revenue.
(*b*) Duties on competitive products.
(*c*) Preference secured by (1) Free List for goods produced within the Empire (as in the tariffs of Canada and New Zealand) or the United Kingdom alone (as in the case of Australia) while duties are retained on similar goods from foreign countries; (2) remission of duty in groups (*a*) and (*b*).

These methods operate separately or in combination.

The outstanding feature of these methods is undoubtedly the adoption of an Empire Free List, and in regard to this method the arrangement between Canada and the West Indies makes a new departure of great importance. In the case of certain items now imported from all countries free of duty, duties of not less than a certain fixed amount are to be imposed when the goods enter Canada from foreign countries, while freedom of entry is to be maintained for goods from the British West Indies and the United Kingdom. It is not clear what is the position of other parts of the Empire in respect of these items, but I suppose it may be presumed that Canada preserves full liberty of action in the matter. It has to be remembered that this development of Empire tariffs has proceeded at a period when the United Kingdom has to take no decisive step in the direction of preference. In these circumstances it is impossible to say what final form Empire tariffs will assume, should the United Kingdom at any time fall into line with what appears to approach a general Empire movement.

The United Kingdom, so far as her tariff policy is concerned, at present stands outside the general Empire movement and she is unable, so long as the present policy prevails, to enter into schemes of mutual Empire preference which have been discussed at successive Imperial Conferences, but if the policy of the United Kingdom were at any time to change, it is presumable that under any scheme of preference which has been suggested by reasonable statesmen in England, tariff advantages would be extended to Indian products. Under the scheme which, so far as is ascertainable, has been generally accepted in responsible circles in the Tariff Reform movement it was held, I believe, that in a recent year £23,000,000 worth of Indian agricultural produce and manufactures would be directly benefited by tariff preferences in the United Kingdom. I do not advance that as my opinion. I merely allude to the opinion held by those who advocate a new departure.

What we have to consider at this stage is not the details of a possible preferential tariff, but rather whether India could, if called upon to join in a great federation of Imperial preferences, respond to that call without sacrificing the essentially revenue character of its Customs schedule. Any such movement would presumably involve, in the first instance at least, a loss of revenue unless we were prepared to raise the general incidence of the tariff from 5 per cent., at which it at present stands, to some higher figure in respect of those articles or countries for which there would be no preferences. That changes of this nature would be difficult, I cannot conceal; that they will be impossible, I do not pretend.

It can be urged that if any changes of this character were adopted in the Indian tariff, India would stand to lose by retaliatory measures on the part of foreign countries which now take so large a proportion of Indian produce. To this the advocates of preferential tariffs might possibly reply that throughout the civilised world there is an increasing tendency to regard preferential tariffs within an empire, however widely scattered, as matters of domestic concern; and that these preferences in fact do not now bar Colonies from participation in the advantages of treaties with foreign countries on the ground of discrimination. Furthermore the character of the exports of India to foreign countries would make it difficult for these foreign countries to retaliate unless the whole construction of their tariffs were modified and they were prepared to inflict damage on their own industries, for India exports to European countries and the United States nearly £50,000,000 worth of merchandise which consists chiefly of raw materials for manufactures, for the most part admitted free of duty, and also of foodstuffs.

The question is far from ripe for decision, and in my reply I merely endeavour to state the pros and cons as impartially as I can.

It would be unfair to my successor to do more.

LETTER XXIII.—TRAINING OF I.C.S., GOKHALE, AND FAREWELL BANQUET

SIMLA, *June 18th*, 1913.

I HAD been but a short time in India when I became greatly impressed by the fact that whilst British officers and English commercial men almost invariably get on very well with Indians, there is not infrequently ill-feeling between Indians and members of the Indian Civil Service. It is quite a common thing to find Indian gentlemen welcomed by English regiments and a well-marked spirit of *bonne camaraderie* existing between the regiment and their Indian friends.

I noticed also that English commercial men speak of Indians as "quite a good sort and all right if you take them the right way."

Doubtless the fact that neither British officers nor commercial men have any direct share in the government of the country has much to do with it, but that alone hardly furnishes a sufficient reason for the difference.

I have come to the conclusion that such friction as exists is partly due to the lack of proper training of young officials when they first take up their duties.

I claim some knowledge of the subject because I instituted a system under which a number of young I.C.S. were called up in turn from the

Provinces to serve under me for a brief period at the Ministry of Finance.

No doubt many Commissioners take especial pains to train their young subordinates not only in their official duties but also in their attitude and tone towards Indians. But some do not, and a cross-grained or neglectful Commissioner can taint the whole staff of his district.

Many young Civil Servants land in India full of enthusiasm, desperately anxious to do their duty, and quite ready to receive the Indian as a fellow-subject and a comrade, but there are also thoroughly promising but somewhat casual beginners who require guidance to turn them into really good officials.

I came across one such at Bombay. He had not long landed and I heard him humming:

> " Oh ! I thank my God for this at least—
> I was born in the West and not in the East,
> And He made me a human instead of a beast
> Whose hide is covered with hair."

A bad beginning, thought I.

I scraped acquaintance with him (he had no notion who I was) and asked him to lunch with me at the Taj. I led him on to tell me all he thought, and gradually I extracted from him his ideas, his intentions, and his aspirations.

I believe he turned out, eventually, an exceptionally promising officer, but I shudder to think of what he might have turned into had he been left entirely dependent for his training on a certain type of Commissioner.

I am convinced that greater attention to the training of young civilians in what I may term the "tone towards Indians" will do more to allay anti-English feeling than anything else. Would that some of the English in India could be brought to realise how much they lose by not gaining the love of their fellow-Indian subjects, who are so well worthy of our respect and affection.

There are *budmashes* in every community and every country is cursed with some disloyal men, but in India both are mere fractions of the whole.

Indians, Mahomedans and Hindoos alike, are generous - minded, trustworthy, and intensely loyal.

If ever England is in a tight place the loyalty of India will not only show, it will blaze forth.

I may be allowed to give my own experience in two instances. When I added somewhat heavily to the import duties it was suggested to me that my Budget secrets should be entrusted to only my highest staff—that is, to Englishmen alone. I declined to adopt the suggestion, and a goodly number of lowly as well as more highly paid Indian officials of the Finance Department acquired full knowledge of my Budget provisions.

Obviously the information was worth much money. Silver came in for its full share of additional duty, but so loyally was my secret kept that the importers of a large quantity of silver on board a ship anchored for some days in Bombay Harbour omitted to clear and were caught by the increased duty.

A Finance Minister from England should arrive in India several months before the presentation of the Budget so as to have time to learn something of the country and to be able to *envisager la situation.*

In my case circumstances beyond my control landed me in Calcutta but a short time before the Budget, and I was hardly able to do more than stare at an appreciable deficit.

It was a wonderful chance for the Indian members of the Legislative Council to upset an inexperienced Minister, and I anticipated a trying time of it in debate. The one man I frankly feared was Gokhale, the Gladstone of India.

Accordingly I endeavoured to find out what Gokhale's line of attack would be. All and everyone told me that the attempt would be futile, and that any apparent frankness on Gokhale's part would only be a cloak to his real intentions. So I left him severely alone.

Imagine my surprise at receiving on the eve of the debate a letter from Gokhale, whom I did not even know, to the effect that as he had good reason to believe that I meant to do my utmost for the good of India, he had no desire to embarrass me, and that he therefore sent me the notes of the speech he proposed to make so that I should not be taken unawares.

I do not believe that such a generous attitude has ever been assumed by the leader of the Opposition in any other country in the world, and I greatly doubt if it ever will be.

I subsequently invited Gokhale to pay me a visit at Peterhof and he stayed with me for a week, a week for me of unalloyed pleasure.

Gokhale always reminds me of Mr. Gladstone,

possessing in my opinion much of the greatness and many of the weaknesses of that statesman.

He said to me when leaving:

"When I go to England I am invited to stay with distinguished men of the political, academic, and literary world, but yours is the first Englishman's roof in India under which I have been invited to sleep."

And yet to converse with Gokhale is at once joy and enlightenment.

Alas! my time is drawing to a close. In a brief period I shall have to leave my beloved India for ever, and mine will be a sore, sore sorrow.

I landed in India unknown to all Indians and I myself knew them not. Their country was a mere geographical expression to me; but from the very first they dealt with me fairly, throughout they dealt with me generously, and after I had been a time in their land they gave me, in full measure, friendship and affection.

I part with them all, highly-placed and lowly, rich and poor, with a heavy heart.

A hard life has made somewhat of a materialist of me, yet at times I experience a weird feeling that when my body ends in corruption my spirit may hover over the sacred river I have learnt to love so well.

A large number of what may justly be termed the best and most distinguished of the Indian community have given me a farewell banquet on the eve of my departure.

Will you think me very egotistical if I send you a report of the speech which I addressed to them on the occasion?

It is the only non-official speech I have as yet ever allowed myself to make during the whole of my five years in India.

You will bear in mind the Oriental atmosphere in which it was delivered.

SPEECH DELIVERED BY SIR GUY FLEETWOOD WILSON AT A FAREWELL BANQUET GIVEN TO HIM AT SIMLA BY THE INDIAN COMMUNITY ON JUNE 17TH, 1913.

INTRODUCTORY.

In my young days it was my privilege to know John Lawrence of the Punjab, or as he was when I knew him, Lord Lawrence, ex-Viceroy of India.

I remember his saying to me in his somewhat rough way:

"The wise man in India never makes a speech; the man who makes a speech in India when he need not do so, is a fool."

Although at that time India was to me but a geographical expression, and I never, in my wildest moments, then anticipated ever visiting India, much less holding office in India, Lord Lawrence's words impressed themselves upon my mind; and when I accepted my present appointment, I determined that nothing should induce me to make a speech during my tenure of office, except such speeches as I should be compelled to make in Council.

I have up to the present never spoken in this country outside the Council, and it was my hope and my intention to leave India without doing so. I find myself, however, in a position to-night which renders it incumbent upon me to break the rule which I had laid down for myself.

I look round this banqueting-hall and I see Indians of nearly every caste, creed, rank, and profession who have come from nearly every part of this great continent to do honour to one who has for the best part of five years endeavoured to do his duty by them; and it would ill become me if I did not endeavour to convey to you all, even though it be very inadequately, my feelings of profound, heartfelt gratitude for your kindness.

I cannot refrain from expressing my regret that so many of you should have been put to the great personal inconvenience entailed by travelling long journeys in hot weather to enable you to come to Simla to do me honour.

The kindness which you are showing me this evening is literally overwhelming, and I do not hesitate to admit that it has affected me to a degree which renders the task of speaking to-night even more difficult than it must of necessity be. Indeed, I hardly think I could have faced the duty of endeavouring to give adequate expression to my gratitude were it not for the fact that I fully appreciate that it is not the individual to whom you are doing honour, but rather the honest effort which has influenced me throughout my Indian career, not only to identify myself with the aspirations of Indians, but to recognise the honest desire which influences them, to combine progress and the desire to share in the Government of their own country, with the most complete and absolute devotion to our common Sovereign and loyalty to the British Empire.

If I have been able, in the short time I have been with you, to impress upon you how earnestly I have hoped to succeed in making myself acquainted with the wishes and the aspirations of Indians; if I have succeeded in impressing upon you that my desire was to meet you with sympathy and understanding and in the spirit of helpfulness, it has been owing rather to the readiness of Indians to give me credit for good intentions than to any successful effort on my part to render them service.

Would that all Englishmen, official and unofficial, could be made to realise how truly Indians believe in the efficacy of good intentions; how ready they are to give credit for those intentions; how appreciative they are of sympathy; how responsive they are to affection, and how foreign it is to their nature to take undue advantage of that brotherly familiarity which between equals cannot be open to misinterpretation.

How true are the words of General Gordon, who died at Khartoum:

"To govern men there is but one way, and it is eternal truth. Get into their skins. Try to realise their feelings. That is the true secret of government."

It is not my wont to indulge in lengthy quotations, but I shall to-night quote extensively, indeed textually, from the utterances of that Viceroy and that statesman who are connected with the grant to India of the first semblance of an assembly empowered to voice public opinion in this country and capable of so doing. I shall adopt the words of others who could speak with authority, not because it is admittedly better to read a good sermon than to preach a bad one, but because it is especially incumbent on me as a member of the Government of India to be exceptionally circumspect lest any utterance of mine admit of being interpreted—or twisted—into even the semblance of a pronouncement of a fresh policy, or the enunciation of new administrative or executive principles.

1908.

When I landed in India at the close of the year 1908 I was appalled by the task which lay before me. It was as complex as it was new to me. I found myself in a country with which I was totally unacquainted. My fellow-countrymen here were as much strangers to me as were the Indians, and I was brought in contact with a race as different from my own as it is possible for two races to be who spring from one common—the Aryan—origin. The only thing which met me with which I had ever before been familiar was a large deficit in the Budget.

I asked myself what hope could I entertain of succeeding in such a task—a task not indeed self-imposed, but undertaken with diffidence and only after having twice declined the proffered honour.

I asked myself the question, "Can I hope to succeed?" and I answered myself, "It is my duty to try," and I was supported by the conviction that if I did my very best I should at least be given credit for an earnest endeavour to acquit myself without discredit and possibly with advantage to those whom I had come to serve.

I have had a very hard life at Home and abroad, and my five years in India have been full of heavy work, of worry and of anxiety, but I have received and am taking away a priceless reward—the esteem and affection of all those Indians with whom I have been brought in contact.

From the first you all gave me a fair chance; from the first you gave me encouragement and support. No one can, I think, charge me with having either flattered you or feared you. I said to myself, "I shall have to hold my own, to utter unpalatable truths, to add to Indian burdens and thereby to incur the odium of both my countrymen and my Indian fellow-subjects." But I also said to myself, " This Indian race seems just, it appears to be sympathetic, and I believe that it will realise that I mean well by them and by India. I shall work for India according to the motto of my family—*fortiter et fideliter*."

I have indeed reaped a full measure of the harvest of reward. I have learnt to love India whole-heartedly, and equally I love Indians, and I should be guilty of base ingratitude were it otherwise.

When I look back on the state of the country as it was when I first came to it, and look upon it now when I am about to leave it, and when I realise the changes which have operated, the progress which has been made, and the marked influence which has been impressed upon the country by the reforms which came into being in 1909, I can hardly believe that the India which I leave is the same India which I found.

I do not propose to-night—it would be quite out of place for me to do so—to deal with the financial position of five years ago as compared with the financial position of to-day. I can only in passing express my thanks to Providence for some good monsoons and consequent bounteous harvests which have enabled me to provide for the expenditure needed for the good government and the development of this country; and I must add that if any success has attended my efforts in dealing with the finances entrusted to my care, it is largely owing to the reasonable, the considerate, and the absolutely fair treatment which I have received at the hands of my Indian Colleagues in the Legislative Council.

Great indeed are the changes which have taken place in that assembly since I first sat in it. Its evolution has been as startling as its success has been undeniable. The first time that I addressed the Council we numbered, I think, twenty-one members, of whom only six were Indians; and the like number only were present when I made my first speech in answer to the criticisms on my first Budget. I remember the day well. It was on the 29th of March, 1909, and the day was abnormally hot and close, even for that time of year in Calcutta. Partly owing to the heat, but largely no doubt owing to the wearisome effect of my first attempt at oratory, one by one every single member present went to sleep; and it is the simple truth that, after awhile, I actually fell asleep myself in the course of the delivery of my statement.

I ask myself what would happen to my successor were he to allow himself, in the forthcoming Session, to go to sleep when defending his Budget? Some of my friends who sat in the last Council have gone, but the incisive criticism of Mr. Gokhale, the torrential eloquence of the pundit Malaviya, the emphatic utterance of Mr. Acharia, to say nothing of the journalistic thunder of Mr. Surendra Nath Banerjee, would soon lead to a rude awakening.

When I look back upon the character of the old Council and consider the quality of the present Council, I am almost astonished that even the old name remains.

In wishing good-bye to the old dispensation, I used these words:

"The reforms which have been decided upon and which will presumably become operative before this time next year will unquestionably vastly increase the labour and the difficulties of the Finance Member.

"I do not fear the change.

"Undoubtedly it will lead to increased and

more searching criticism, but I believe that the criticism will be the outcome not of an intention to embarrass a public servant who is honestly trying to do his duty, but rather of a desire to help him to effect improvement.

"I shall welcome criticism because I believe my critics will be actuated by the same impulse, the same desire, which will influence me—a common desire to improve the work of those who govern and the conditions of those who have to bear taxation."

1912.

In my words of welcome to the new dispensation, I said:

"I may confidently say that that forecast has been fully realised. It is not the time to sum up the influence which this Council has exercised on the general administration of India, or to estimate the services which it has rendered alike to the rulers and to the ruled. But I can testify unhesitatingly to the power that the Council holds for good in directing attention to the finances of the country, in scrutinising expenditure, and in advising the Government on the employment of the public funds. I have always found the criticisms of my non-official colleagues temperate, suggestive, and helpful. Unable though we may at times have been to accept their opinions at once, they have not been without their effect on our subsequent arrangements; and even where we wholly disagreed, they have shown us fresh points of view and warned us of probable dangers. It is no exaggeration to say that the free interchange of views which this Council stimulates has already become a powerful factor for good in the financial policy of India."

THE REFORMED COUNCIL.

Up to two years ago my connection with the Council was primarily financial. During the last two years, however, I have been very much more closely connected with the Council owing to the honour conferred on me by the Viceroy which has empowered me to preside at its deliberations as His Excellency's representative.

When presiding over any assembly, it is easier to note its character, to gauge the value of its work, and to appreciate the tone which pervades it, more fully than is possible during an active participation in the actual debating; and I think I can speak with some assurance, and that I may hold that my judgment of the Council is the outcome of greater experience of it than that of anyone else in this country. I have no hesitation in saying that our Legislative Council bears the most favourable comparison with the best analogous assemblies in other countries, and I am well acquainted with many, and that it is immeasurably superior to the remainder. The eloquence of some of its members is of the highest order; the single-minded desire to further the interests of the country is universal; and the determination to respect the rulings of the chair so as to maintain good order in debate and uphold the honour and good name of the Council, is as conspicuous as it is successful.

Important classes among you—I quote Lord Morley — representing ideas that have been fostered and encouraged by British rule claim equality of citizenship and a greater share in legislation and government. The politic satisfaction of such a claim will strengthen, not impair, existing authority and power; and a marked step towards the satisfaction of that claim was taken when the decision was arrived at to confer on India the Reformed Council.

By inviting the leaders of Indian public opinion to become fellow-workers with us in British administration, and by securing the representation of those important interests and communities which go to form the real strength of India, we have borne in mind, as Lord Morley has told us, the hopes held out to the people of India in Queen Victoria's Proclamation of 1858. And Lord Morley has added: "We have felt that the political atmosphere of a bureaucracy may become close and confined, and that the admittance of air is beneficial to its health and strength. I defy anyone to show that the admittance of air has been otherwise than beneficial not only to the bureaucracy but also to the leaders of public opinion in this country." It was Lord Morley who expressed the belief that in the fellow-service of British and Indian administrators under a supreme Government is the key to the future political happiness of this country. I may echo his words and say with him that it is in that belief that I have worked hard for India, and that I have worked hard to make the Legislative Council a success; and when I see around me to-day the representatives of powerful communities and interests which are represented in that Council, and know that they are here to testify their appreciation of such service as I have been able to render, then indeed I feel that not in vain has the bread been cast upon the waters.

I can assuredly bear witness that England is reaping, and will continue to reap, her reward for the generous impulse which has conferred on India a Reformed Council and has enabled Indians to voice their opinions with freedom and with authority.

The Result of Education.

In 1909 and again in 1910 Lord Minto gave utterance to two weighty statements.

"Indian affairs," he said, "and the methods of Indian administration have never attracted more public attention in India and at home than at the present moment. The reasons for their doing so are not far to seek. The growth of education, which British rule has done so much to encourage, is bearing fruit. Important classes of the population are learning to realise their own position, to estimate for themselves their own intellectual capacities, and to compare their claims, for an equality of citizenship, with those of a ruling race, whilst the directing influences of political life at home are simultaneously in full accord with the advance of political thought in India.

"We, the Government of India, cannot shut our eyes to present conditions. The political atmosphere is full of change, questions are before us which we cannot afford to ignore, and which we must attempt to answer."

And he recognised that politically India is in a transition state; that new and just aspirations are springing up amongst its people, which the ruling power must be prepared not only to meet but to assist. "A change is rapidly passing over the land, and we cannot afford to dally. And to my mind," he added, "nothing would be more unfortunate for India than that the Government of India should fail to recognise the signs of the times."

What was true then is equally true now. You cannot set back the hands of the clock, and we should combine to ensure its keeping true time. You are not justified in forcing the pace; but neither should we be right in jamming back the regulator to the extreme point of slow. Let us not forget—

> "With what a leaden and retarding weight
> Does expectation load the wings of time."

It is incessantly being impressed upon me that a prolonged residence in the country is an essential condition to any knowledge of India. Doubtless in India as elsewhere intimacy with the inhabitants, topographical knowledge, and personal experience of the special conditions which prevail, present inestimable advantages, but after all human nature is human nature all the world over.

It is the wider knowledge of the world rather than the restricted knowledge of India which I have so often found lacking in those who have to guide the destinies of this country. How completely a man who has never set foot on Indian soil can grasp the fundamental principles which govern some of our difficulties is well exemplified in Lord Morley. Would thirty years' residence in India have enabled him to express with greater accuracy or more precision the movement with which here we are so conversant and which he himself has defined as a living movement in the mind of the peoples, a movement for objects which we ourselves have taught them to think desirable objects, and he goes on to say in that perfect English of which he is master: "Much of this movement arises from the fact that there is now a large body of educated Indians who have been fed, at our example and our instigation, upon some of the great teachers and masters of this country—Milton, Burke, Macaulay, Mill, and Spencer. Surely it is a mistake in us not to realise that these masters should have mighty force and irresistible influence. Who can be surprised that educated Indians who read those high masters and teachers of ours are intoxicated with the ideas of freedom, nationality, self-government, that breathes the breath of life in those inspiring and illuminating pages? Who of us that had the privilege in the days of our youth, at college or at home, of turning over those golden chapters, and seeing that lustrous firmament dawn over youthful imaginations,—who of us can forget, shall I call it the intoxication and rapture, with which we strove to make friends with truth, knowledge, beauty, freedom? Then why should we be surprised that young Indians feel the same movement of mind when they are made free of our own immortals?"

You often hear people talk of the educated section of the people of India as a mere handful—an infinitesimal fraction. So they are in numbers; but it is fatally idle to say that this infinitesimal fraction does not count. This educated section is making and will make all the difference. That they would sharply criticise the British system of government has been long known. It was inevitable. There need be no surprise in the fact that they want a share in political influence, and want a share in the emoluments of administration.

But while I declare to you with all the emphasis at my command that these words once uttered, these pledges once made, by responsible Englishmen, are going to be kept, I must also ask you to grant me an old man's privilege while I say something in the way both of counsel and of encouragement to you in your present difficulties and perplexities—difficulties which I appreciate with a deep and sincere sympathy.

My counsel is this: Do not condemn our English honesty and veracity if you find that we move very slowly forward towards the goal of your hopes. Do not mistake that slowness for want of faith. Do not suppose for a moment that we are going to be false to our word. It is not this which is taking place, however much at times it may wear that outward appearance. Believe me, it is simply the working out of our somewhat stolid English nature, which has made political caution a part of our very blood. We cannot change our nature any more than you can change yours. You are much quicker emotionally than we are: you are a very emotional people: you are in many respects also intellectually quicker. That is your nature and you may well be proud of it. But try to understand ours: for we also are proud of our nature. We do wish to be absolutely honourable in our conduct towards India. That is a part of our conception of an English gentleman. But you will always find us politically hesitating and almost overcautious. We test one step, time after time, before we take another; and even then we are not satisfied and fear we have been imprudent. That is our nature: it has become a kind of political creed with us, what the poet has called—

> "Freedom slowly broadening down
> From precedent to precedent."

Again my counsel is this: Do not be surprised at all this caution, but expect it from us and never look for anything else, or you will be disappointed.

And I would add, if you will allow me as your friend and guest to-night, a word of personal explanation, a confession of my own faith about India. It is this: If I were convinced, from my five crowded years of Indian experience, that this English political caution which is a part of our English nature were standing in the way of India's progress, then I should be a pessimist. But I am nothing of the kind. On the contrary, I believe that this very quality of English nature is promoting the progress of India and not retarding it. India, with its age-long traditions and its store-house of treasures to be preserved for mankind at large, is not like a small South American Republic where a violent revolution is a kind of hot-weather relaxation. Stability and settlement in this country mean everything. India, with all the memories of the pillage and rapine of the eighteenth century behind her, cannot afford to go back to a time of unsettlement and anarchy. Every year of settlement and peace is a year to the good: it makes for Indian unity, Indian solidarity, and Indian prosperity: it affords a means by which India may give out her own great intellectual and spiritual treasures to the world. But let anarchy once come in; let hasty steps in government be taken which may lead to anarchy: let the present steady but slow progress be interrupted, and then no one can tell in this vast continent whether the spark once kindled may not light a vast and awful conflagration. In India we are not dealing with an insignificant country where a false step or a hasty experiment may be easily rectified. We are dealing with one-fifth of the human race; and, therefore, for the sake of the peace of mankind, for the sake of the prosperity of mankind, for the sake of the higher intellectual welfare of mankind we must move slowly; we must give no countenance to anything which will lead to anarchy or even to revolution; we must set our hopes wholly and solely on steady and ordered progress.

For this reason, therefore, I believe with all my heart that this quality of political circumspection in our rule, corresponding with our somewhat English temperament, is a blessing to India at the present time and not a curse. I know how galling it must be at times to some of the finest emotional instincts in Indian nature, instincts which I admire; but I would ask you to take long views instead of short views. By all means urge us on when we go too slow; by all means criticise us in the freest friendly spirit in Council and in the Public Press; but never distrust us; never lose confidence; above all, never despond. I do not ask you to be optimistic; but I do ask you not to be pessimistic; I do ask you to have a steady confidence in our rule based on a steady belief in our honour. We shall not in the long run disappoint you; only you must give us time. Help us to the uttermost in preserving and conserving the forces of stability and order; help us to keep firm the bases of law and authority on which in the end all constitutional government must rest; help us to make clear to young and ardent spirits which are the hope of a great people that we are moving towards a high and worthy goal—a goal which will include all that is greatest and best in India's past; help us to do this, and keep your own confidence unshaken and immovable, and you will be the truest benefactors of your country.

The Present Situation.

We are face to face in India with a situation which is novel and which may be embarrassing; but I cannot account it dangerous. It will become so only if it be handled intemperately.

It has come upon both rulers and ruled with startling suddenness. The former must not resent; the latter need not exult.

We shall have to resort to the more difficult arts of persuasion and conciliation, in the place of the easier methods of autocracy; and you will have to remember that if you have qualified for government it is to us that you owe your training.

Difficulties beset your path and ours, but I have no fear for the future. I have complete confidence in the progress of this great country; in the regeneration of the Indian people. I have confidence, absolute and illimitable, in what is even dearer to my heart: in good-will between your race and mine; in mutual respect and affection between English and Indian.

It was your King-Emperor himself who brought you a message of sympathy and of hope.

The atmosphere has changed from dark and sullen to hopeful. Let East and West combine to allow naught to overcloud that promising sky.

Conclusion.

We are going through a period of transition, and such a time carries with it a heavy load of anxiety. The burden will lie heavily on my Colleagues of the great Civil Service, to whom modern India owes its very existence. I know full well how heavy that burden can be.

But to him who is called upon to share in the government of this country, I say, take to heart, as I have done, the words of the Psalmist:

> " He that hath clean hands and a pure heart, who hath not lifted up his soul unto vanity; nor sworn deceitfully:
>
> " He shall receive the blessing from the Lord and righteousness from the God of his salvation."

To my fellow-Indian subjects I say, be of good cheer, the Government of India is the heritage of no bureaucracy; it is the heritage of English statesmanship, and the heart of England is sound on this great question of Indian progress. Have confidence in the assurance given you by the Viceroy, whom your King-Emperor has appointed to rule this country, in almost the first words he spoke when he rose from a bed of suffering and of sorrow:

" I will pursue without faltering the same policy in the future as during the past two years, and I will not waver a hair's-breadth from that course.

" My faith in India, its future, and its people remains unshaken."

Answer him: " We abide in your faith; we know you will not fail us."

Let both races repeat in unison the prayer of our late King-Emperor:

" May Divine protection and favour strengthen the wisdom and mutual good-will that are needed for the achievement of a task as glorious as was ever committed to rulers and subjects in any State or Empire of recorded time."

As for myself; it but remains for me to give expression to one all-inspiring aspiration: May India, the India that I love, become a land, in the words of Rabindranath Tagore:

" Where the mind is without fear and the head is held high;
Where knowledge is free;
Where the world has not been broken up into fragments by narrow domestic walls;
Where words come out from the depth of truth;
Where tireless striving stretches its arms towards perfection;
Where the clear stream of reason has not lost its way into the dreary desert sand of dead habit;
Where the mind is led forward by Thee into ever-widening thought and action—
Into that heaven of freedom, my Father, let this country awake."

LETTER XXIV.—LAST SHOOT

SIMLA, *June 21st*, 1913.

DURING the melancholy process of packing I have come upon this letter, written three months ago, which for some unknown reason eluded the mail.

April 21st, 1913.—This is the first time since the Delhi drama that I have been able to absent myself from the seat of government, which is a grandiloquent manner of saying it is the first occasion on which I have been able to allow myself a ten days' holiday.

It is to that good sportsman and excellent Forest Officer James William Best, Lord Wynford's son,* that I owe my last shot at a tiger. He arranged the expedition for me, my last in India.

I left Delhi on April 4th for Bisalpur, in the Central Provinces, where the heat was almost past bearing; central India is just now a fiery furnace. Best met me and we started on our twenty-four mile elephant ride, reaching the camp at 6 in the afternoon. My tent was very comfortable, but water was scanty and bad, our soda-water having gone astray.

The camp, situated in Khondra Forest, was not very far from a pool surrounded by black rocks, the approach to it reminding me somewhat of the Glen of Weeping, Glencoe.

* See Appendix I.

Tigers frequent the pool, and on the 8th Best and I had a very quiet stalk in the hope of coming upon one.

We got to the pool just in time to get a glimpse of a tiger who had been having a swim, but not in time to get a shot at him.

On the 10th we received news of a " kill " and tried to stalk two tigers who had lain up near it, but they got our wind and slunk off.

This stalking on foot in intense heat with only almost undrinkable water available I found very exhausting.

During our stalks we had but one companion, a really first-class shikari who was also an excellent tracker.

On the 11th we were again defeated by a wary tiger, but the 12th proved our lucky day.

We got on the track of a tiger about 10 in the morning and followed it along a dry nullah—that is, a dry watercourse. The nullah was deep and narrow between high banks of red-hot rocks, the refracted heat from which almost stifled us. I had taken the precaution to wrap cotton-wool all over the steel frame of my glasses, but even so they worried me a good deal, as the glass itself was so hot as to affect my eyesight. I could not handle my rifle without gloves.

Occasionally the river-bed was obstructed by large boulders of rock, and as we did our utmost to creep along as noiselessly as possible, we ran considerable risk of coming suddenly and without the least warning on the tiger that we knew was in front of us.

After two hours of heavy walking in scorching

heat we reached a circular sunken hollow, which in the rainy season had been a deep pool, surrounded by rocks some 20 feet high.

Here the shikari halted us and pointed to a relatively small hole in the rock about 15 feet above us, from which a narrow, shelf-like path led to the forest above.

" *The bagh* is resting in there," said the shikari.

The three of us stood close together in the centre of the pit, for it was little else, with our eyes glued on the hole which was the entrance to Mrs. Tiger's apartment.

It was against all rule to fire at her when several feet above us, as it was an absolute certainty that the shot would bring her down on the top of us; and that is just what happened.

After about two minutes of, for us, intense strain the tigress came out of the cave. We fired almost simultaneously, but I am of opinion that Best fired a second or two before me and hit her first, thus earning the skin, which, however, he most generously insisted on my keeping.

What happened after we fired I am unable to describe with exactitude. The tiger came down amongst us, and I have a recollection of gravel flying about and of a certain amount of concentrated essence of tension prevailing, but Best was as cool as the proverbial cucumber and it was his finishing shot which killed her. She was dying when she came into us, but quite able and willing to make things unpleasant for all concerned.

I rested a couple of days in camp and learnt to appreciate Best's sterling qualities and I hope we shall remain fast friends.

According to my invariable practice, I myself cleaned my beloved rifle after I got into camp and replaced it in its case.

I confess without shame that as I suddenly realised that I did so for the last time a sob escaped me.

(This day week I sail from Bombay.)

LETTER XXV.—INDIAN UNREST

BOMBAY, *June 29th*, 1913.

IN one of my earliest letters to you I dwelt on what, to make it palatable, is termed Indian unrest.

Some years have passed since then; my experience has increased, my observation has been prolonged, and my consideration of the subject constant.

Perhaps you may be interested in a later expression of my views on the subject.

In Europe and in America there is a marked tendency on the part of the labour and lower middle class to take an entirely new view of life. They have realised that they do not enjoy to so full an extent as do those in the superior *couches sociales* the good things of this world. Not only have they set themselves to think out the reason for this distinction, but they have at the same time devoted their thoughts to the correction, at almost any cost to the community as a whole, of what quite naturally presents itself to them as an indefensible state of affairs.

In India also, a new view of life is presenting itself to the people. With the rapid and wholesale increase in intercommunication, the spread of knowledge born of Western education, and the self-reliance created by a more accurate knowledge of Western conditions, there has radiated from the educated Indians a sense of undue subordination to an alien race. The position was admirably summed up by Sir Krishna Gupta in a lecture delivered in England in 1911: "While there is a growing consciousness in India of the inevitable drawbacks of alien rule, there is also a widespread conviction that national salvation can be attained under the fostering care and guidance of Britain. The best minds among the Indians eagerly gaze towards the goal bringing her on the level of the self-governing Colonies, so that she may take her place in the Empire not as a mere dependency but on terms of equality and co-ordination."

Using the term "unrest" in its usual acceptation, I think it may justly be held that unrest divides itself into two classes: impulsive unrest and resultant unrest. I cannot think of more suitable definitions.

The first is often difficult to account for. It is generally the outcome of that peculiar "sudden impulse" which resulted in the Crusades, in the migration of certain Russian religious communities and in unexpected revolts often arising out of trivialities. The second is very different. It is usually the effect of prolonged and often misdirected thought, tending to dwell upon and develop a sense of injury.

In a population comprising hundreds of millions the ground is fallow for the development of both classes of unrest and both must be anticipated. They will raise their head at times, and in all probability for all time in the East to an even greater extent than in the West.

It is most important, therefore, not to be carried

away by the belief when sporadic outbursts occur in India that the whole country is in a state of revolt.

Distance tends to produce such impression.

Dining quietly in London, you learn with equanimity that there have been serious riots in Liverpool, but if you happen to be in Portugal at the time and read the news in the Portuguese newspapers you almost allow yourself to believe that England is ablaze from Sutherland to Cornwall.

It is important to realise this tendency when reading newspaper accounts, possibly quite accurate, of riots in India.

What is essential is to check any such upheavals firmly but so temperately, so judicially, as to prevent anything approaching a sense of tyranny and government by the sword, which would result in a uniform mental attitude in the loyal and the moderate, the disloyal and the extremists.

You have both classes in India as elsewhere.

So long as you do nothing to drive the former into the arms of the latter, you need apprehend no real danger to the solidarity of the Anglo-Indian Empire. The real danger which confronts us lies in a policy of alternate repression and concession, a refusal to grant reforms ungrudgingly *and in time*, and a failure to fully recognise the inevitable effect of our own introduction into India of Western education and Western ideals.

Treat India as in the past you have treated Ireland and you will have to face a second Ireland, but an Ireland represented by a huge continent and one of the largest populations in the world.

Should that contingency arise, you will have to

reconquer India. I firmly believe that we could, but how shall we stand when we have done so?

In the distant past we governed India by the sword. There was then no alternative. We cannot, and we assuredly have no wish to do so, in the future.

That we honestly desire the good-will of Indians is indisputable, that we can retain it I have no doubt whatever, but we can only do so by keeping constantly and prominently before us the right of Indians to a place in the sun.

One of our greatest assets is the Indians' devotion to their Sovereign. It is almost a religion, and this makes it imperative never to allow the influence of the Sovereign to be used to "bolster up" an incompetent Viceroy or to "whitewash" the failures of self-seeking politicians at home.

Twice only, outside Council, have I made a public speech in India. At a farewell banquet given to me by the leading citizens of all races in Bombay I thus preached the gospel of good-will:

"These will be my farewell words in public before leaving this land of memories and regrets. No one could possibly go away unmoved from India after sharing the burden of its hopes and fears, and each word of farewell has become harder and harder to utter. For this dear country that I leave has had a strange and powerful attraction for me. Every phase of its life, from the simple village peasant or the patient brave shikari, to keen intellectual Indians in the different ranks and professions whom I have learnt to call my friends—every phase of this manifold Indian life has become more and more endeared to me. And bound up with these delightful memories there are also recollections equally dear of my own fellow-countrymen—men who have laboured side by side with me and those also whom I have met on my official tours, men who go on working cheerfully year in, year out, under condition of climate and environment which try the strongest constitutions and the most placid nerves.

"As an Englishman I am proud of the achievement that has been wrought in India, under British rule, by the co-operation of English and Indians in the common work of administration. The nineteenth century in India, in spite of all miscarriages and mistakes, is one of the noblest pages in the history of the modern world. The lives of great men like Elphinstone, Bentinck, and the Lawrences, of men like Ram Mohan Roy, Syed Ahmad Khan, and Ranade, to mention only a few names out of a thousand, are still fresh and powerful among us and their influence has made the modern India we know to-day. To them and men like them, we owe the fact that social order reigns over this vast continent, and also that in India during the past three generations one of the most marked intellectual revolutions in the history of mankind has taken place.

"My earliest and happiest impressions of this country were received in this beautiful city of Bombay—surely one of the most beautiful for situation on the face of the whole earth. I found here a kindliness, a liberality, a friendly equality between man and man of all races which has been a joy to me to witness. Indeed, this equality of a common citizenship, which you seem to have achieved in such abundant measure in Bombay, I regard as one of the most significant factors of the present Indian situation, and one of the happiest omens for British rule in India in the future.

"It has been our good-fortune to share together,

owing to good monsoons, sound finance and other causes, an almost unprecedented prosperity, and it may be said, I believe with accuracy, that India to-day is in a sounder financial position than at any other period within the memory of man. I trust that this condition will be maintained, for upon it will depend in a great measure the elimination of those painful and alarming features which have at times tended to mar the harmony and good-will which are taking so firm a root on Indian soil.

" In the Northern Provinces of India, especially in the Punjab, a development has set in which should make those lands almost the richest granaries of Asia, and afford scope also for the rise of large and important industries among the sturdy and practical northern races of India. The rapid absorption of gold in the Punjab is one of the most interesting and remarkable economic features of our age. It may be some time before this new wealth percolates through and finds its proper level among the people as a whole. Prices and wages may be difficult to adjust all at once, and hardships and trouble may occur during their adjustment. But when the transition period is over there can be no question that a great future awaits the Punjab. Its physical resources are very great, and its virile people are developing modern methods of production and distribution. The natural outlet of the exports of the North must be the Western Coast. Bombay as the first and Karachi as the second gate of India will profit largely by each fresh agricultural and industrial expansion, and both will receive an abundant share of the new wealth that is accumulating in Northern India. But more than wealth is wanted in India. What is wanted in India is light, more light, always light, and it is education alone which will give us that light.

"It is to education that we must look to dispel many of the misapprehensions which go so far as to create discontent in this country. Education dispelled the 'money drain theory,' and we must use it to dispel the idea that British rule has reduced India to poverty and its people to starvation. The exact opposite is the case.

"India is at the present time very prosperous and its people have probably never before been so well off. The volume of our exports and imports proves it.

"We have all of us, English and Indian alike, passed through very serious and anxious times.

"The lesson that I have learnt is the supreme importance of trust and confidence in the Indian people, and the assurance that if that trust is firm and that confidence upheld there will inevitably follow a rich harvest of loyalty and affection.

"And I say with conviction, that among those most responsive to such trust I place the educated Indian community.

"Let the appeal be made to trust and confidence —trust and confidence answering to trust and confidence—and there is nothing that educated Indians will not do, there is no sacrifice they will not make for the maintenance of British rule.

"I believe the time has come when an appeal will have to be made for that trust and confidence to the educated classes. It is incumbent on us to ask them with frankness to share our responsibilities in a far greater measure than ever before. They are the true interpreters of the ideals of our rule, and as the elementary education of the masses goes forward the need of loyal and sympathetic interpretation of our aims and objects will be far more important in the future than it has been in the past.

"I leave India to-morrow with the conviction,

hard to analyse but strong and inspiring, that the darkest days are over. Heavy thunder-clouds may gather again as they have done in the past, but they will gather only to be dispersed as the true end of British rule develops and becomes more clearly understood. Each year of settled government that passes, each widening of inter-communication between India and the rest of the world, each successful solution of the problem of Indian Finance, bringing with it increasing prosperity, each exercise of the new responsibilities placed upon Indians themselves in the administration of their own country must make for orderly evolution, contentment, and progress. The common sense of the peoples of India on the one hand, and the sober political instincts of those in authority on the other, will work in the same direction. Only let there be more mutual trust, more mutual confidence, more mutual good-will, for these are the bonds with which the fabric of every great empire is strengthened; and their need is greatest to-day, as their power is strongest to-day, in this great Indian Empire."

Although starting for Home, I shall post this to you, as I intend to go round by sea to London and thence to Germany for a cure.

LETTER XXVI.—ADEN

ADEN, *July 3rd*, 1913.

ADEN marks the confines of the Indian Government, and the privilege is accorded to members of Council to retain their status, and mercifully their salary, until they leave that station on their journey home.

I send you *un petit mot* to let you know that just one hour ago I ceased to be a member of the Government of India (and one or two other things besides) and relapsed into

A NOBODY.

L'ENVOI

THE following verses appeared in the *Pioneer* of June 30th, 1911. They seem so applicable to my own case that I venture to assume the author's and the editor's permission to quote them:

ICHABOD.

"The picture of horse and places,
The tiger-skins spread in the hall,
The *Asian's* reports of old races,
The antlers of stags on the wall:
What dreams of dead days do they waken?
What visions of past they recall?
But what use to repine? I have taken
My leave of it all.

"What can I now turn to for pastime?
I know, in mean streets as I walk,
That I've looked on it all for the last time:
The dripping laborious stalk,
The panther kill claw-marked and bitten,
The pug-marks fresh oozing in mud,
The trail of the tiger lung smitten,
All frothy with blood.

"The bells of the cattle returning
At evening, the cry of the shepherd,
The smoke of the undergrowth burning,
The wood-sawing call of the leopard,
The beat, when the elephants' crashing
Grows steadily nearer and louder:
The fall of the trees they are smashing,
The swing of the howdah.

* * * * *

"The rifles lie idle in cases,
The spear-heads are eaten with rust,
Old age leaves indelible traces:
Life now is but ashes and dust—
I'm weary of vain recollection,
Youth, nerve, and digestion have fled,
But cheer up! There's one saving reflection.
Some day I'll be dead."

J. C. F.

APPENDIX I

"SHIKAR NOTES"

BY THE HON. J. W. BEST, O.B.E.

SHOOTING tigers on foot is the cream of sport; it requires knowledge of the locality, careful planning, crafty stalking, good shooting, and, in addition, entails considerable hardship in enduring the heat. Occasionally risks have to be taken if the tiger is to be bagged. I was once told off to help a distinguished official* to stalk a tiger. The kill was taken as arranged, but the tiger was not by the water, so we went on to a cave which was half-way up the side of a precipitous *khad* and about a stone's-throw distance from where we were standing in the bottom of the *nala*. There was no other way of getting a view of the cave, and the risk of having the tiger come out on top of us had to be taken. We managed to get a stone into the larger mouth of the cave, but not into a small bolt-hole. Nothing happened, so we sat down to rest. Suddenly the shikari showed us a tigress trying to squeeze herself out of the bolt-hole, which she eventually succeeded in doing, and in running up a path towards the top of the *khad*. Two shots were ineffectual, but the third, which broke her forearm, brought her down

* Rt. Hon. Sir Guy Fleetwood Wilson, G.C.I.E., K.C.B., K.C.M.G.

like a rabbit on the side of a hill, and as we thought dead. Half-way down she fetched up against a clump of bamboos, which was fortunate for us, as we were directly below her; we fired a shot at her resting there and found her very much alive. She came on rolling down while we took shooting-gallery shots at her, and eventually finished her off at our feet with a shot in the head. Moral—keep above dangerous game.

APPENDIX II

THE SUNDERBUNDS

"RAOUL" writes in the *Indian Field*:

"I have read with interest your contributor Simba's article on 'Tiger-Shooting in the Sunderbunds,' in your issue of the 25th November.

"As all the shooting-ground alluded to by S. is not far out from Port Canning, I am not surprised that the game he mentions as having seen or heard about was very limited.

"Tigers are perhaps as plentiful now as they were half a century ago. A few tigers are annually killed by native 'shikarees' for the sake of the reward, and fewer still fall to the gun of the sportsman of the West. The impenetrableness of the cover and the difficulty of the ground make the pursuit of these big felines a very difficult and hazardous matter. Owing to the innumerable number of creeks and water-ways, and the treacherous nature of the ground, elephants cannot possibly be used in the Sunderbunds in the pursuit of tigers. Most of these are to be found nowadays, not in what I should call the middle Sunderbunds, with its mangroves and forests of Soonder trees, but where the ground is generally low and under water during the flood-tides. A fair number of tigers may also be found towards the more northern parts of the Sunderbunds, bordering on such parts that have been reclaimed and brought under cultivation, and it is here also that most of the man-eaters are to be found. Almost all Sunderbund tigers are confirmed fearless man-eaters, and those that for some cause or other have been brought once into contact with men are specially so. The southern parts of the Sunderbunds face the sea, and consist mostly of sand-dunes, overgrown in parts with tamarisk and hurtall palms, with an undergrowth of a fine kind of grass, on which large herds of spotted deer may be seen feeding of an early morning or towards evening. Numbers of pigs may be seen here rooting for crabs and roots, as the kind of grass that grows among the sand-dunes has a sort of small bulb to which pigs are very partial. It is in such parts, too, that tigers delight in making their homes, for the large number of deer and pigs, that are to be found about here, supplies them with abundant fare."